A Plateful of SHELLS

"I DON'T EAT BAIT"

A Norwegian author and two Norwegian chefs so sincerely dedicated to cooking and enjoying shellfish may seem a paradox. Until recently, few Norwegians ever considered eating mollusks.

The Norwegian coastal culture has always been restrictive in its use of products of the sea. The diet was, and still is in many places, based on only a few kinds of fish prepared in a few traditional ways. As long as there was enough herring, cod and pollack, that covered the population's basic nutritional and caloric needs. They were seldom prepared in any creative or interesting way, and the variety and wealth of species in the sea was rarely mirrored on the dinner table. Monkfish, wolffish and eel were considered trash fish, and most flat fish were tossed back into the sea. Grey gurnard, garfish and many others were considered inedible. Mussels and other bivalves were used as bait, at best . . . but we have traveled – and learned, eaten mussels in Spain, loved oysters in France, tried clam chowder in the US, enjoyed clams and conch in China. And our eyes have been opened to the fact that we are standing with our feet planted in one big, rich pantry – the Norwegian coast.

Fortunately, consumers are now moving in the right direction. Shellfish are no longer just bait. They are on their way to becoming an enriching and exciting part of our diet. And supply and demand always go together – closely linked to information, knowledge and curiosity. As the selection and availability improve, curiosity will be stimulated. Demand increases, and that initiates a positive cycle. We feel that this book can contribute to this positive and exciting process. We have tried to convey basic knowledge, about how to obtain the ingredients, how to handle, store, clean and use them to their maximum potential – with recipes which range from very simple basics to new and exciting suggestions for preparing all the different kinds of bi-

We are all here – ready to start cleaning shellfish, cutting and chopping ingredients and garnishes, cooking, frying, steaming and broiling. We discuss the dishes, fine-tune the recipes, key all details into the computer, prepare the dishes and photograph them. The kitchen at the Norwegian Seafood Centre gradually turns into an exciting, colorful, and delicious smelling witch's cauldron. These are intense working days for both publisher, chefs, authors, photographer and assistant.

valves. It is important to learn as much as possible about the distinctive qualities of each and their possibilities, how they can be used and why.

"Dish and beverage" harmony

More and more people are interested in learning the best combinations of food and drink. The selection of drinks has developed at an almost explosive rate over the past few years. A good selection of water and mineral water, a steadily increasing selection of beer, and an impressive range of affordable wines give us a wealth of opportunities – but perhaps also more problems when we are standing there trying to make the "right" choice. But there is no "right" choice! There are always many alternatives, and always something which will be just all right, good, or even perfect. The choice of drink with seafood depends upon culture, occasion, budget and personal preference. But most of us who enjoy food have probably experienced both the highs and the lows, that the contents of our glasses can both enhance and detract from the food being served. We have tried to use our own experiences to give some simple advice which can help guide you in matching drinks with shellfish.

Ideas, contents and inspiration - how to read a recipe

Cookbooks can be divided into many categories – from those made to impress colleagues to really basic books with everyday food. Even if this represents a wide range, they have one thing in common – the desire to convey the joy of eating and information about food and its preparation. The way people read a cookbook varies a lot, too. Users range from the reader who leafs through the book, gets hungry just looking at the pictures and goes to a restaurant to eat, to the exacting reader who reads through the recipe ahead of time and plans purchases in detail and follows the recipe to the letter, to the one who sits with the book on

Friday evening seeking inspiration for an improvised dinner the next day.

When we have chosen dishes and written recipes for this book, we have always taken into consideration that the recipes have to fulfill many functions. We have tried hard to make certain that the recipes are accurate and fullproof. You ought to be able to follow the recipes from start to finish and end up with a successful result. But we also hope that these recipes inspire the readers to do their own experiments in the kitchen – that we and our recipes put readers on the right track to dishes which they can call their own specialties, when they serve them to their guests.

Some dishes cannot even be described correctly. A good example of this is risotto. There are as many recipes for this dish as there are housewives in the Po valley. Here, personal preferances play a major role – some like their risotto soft and thoroughly cooked, while others prefer it "al dente" and soft, while others like it a little drier. The same can be said about the phrase "season to taste" which could be salt, pepper or herbs. Where it has been natural to give precise measurements, we have done so, but again, in most cases, it is a question of taste. And here we are at the core of all food preparation: you do not serve food you haven't tasted. Always have a spoon or two handy for tasting. Does the sauce have a well-rounded flavor and enough acidity? Does it need a little sugar, a pinch of salt or a few turns of the pepper mill? When the plate has been set down in front of your guests, you want to be sure that everything tastes good!

All recipes, unless otherwise noted, should serve four. Most are appetizers and snacks, but it is important to remember that shellfish dishes can be served as main courses (just add more) or combined with other seafood. In some places we have given a few suggestions, but it is important that you use our recipes as a departure point and do

your own thing. We hope that you – and your guests – have many good experiences that begin with this book.

Otherwise, it is the result of a combination of creative work and good professional expertise – within completely different fields. We have gotten good advice and help along the way. Our thanks to The Culinary Institute of Norway , which has supplied many recipes, to colleagues who have stepped in when time got the better of us, both at The Culinary Institute and at Terra Bar and Restaurant. A special thanks to Hans Petter Uleberg, who contributed the text about how to read a recipe, and to Arne Duinker at the Institute of Nutrition of the Directorate of Fisheries for suggestions for the manuscript.

When committed savages work together as a team, they need to keep tabs on one another, but not too closely...just enough, so that the most intriguing photograph can be paired with the most interesting text, as a background for the most exciting recipes, with a little information mixed in. We have learned a lot doing this book, and we hope that you will too.

We dedicate this book and the recipes in it to our wives, who have had to live with us throughout this project – we hope that you will get to sample these dishes too one day.

May 2000
Stein Mortensen – Morten Schakenda
Charles Tjessem – Per Eide

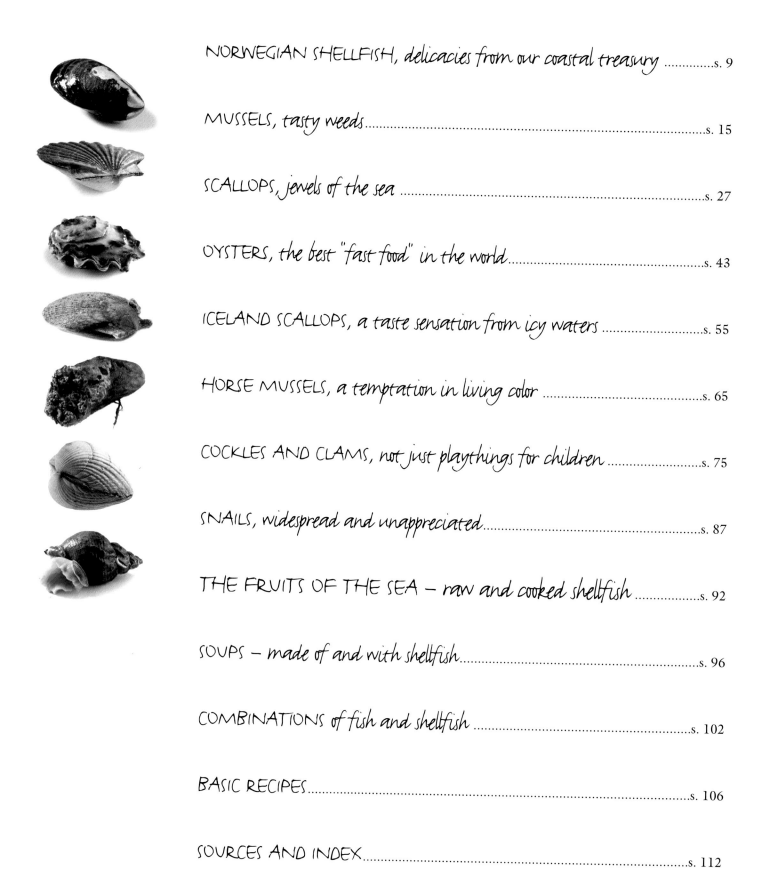

Publisher and copyright:
KOM Forlag as, Vågeveien 10, 6509 Kristiansund
Telefone (+47) 71 67 83 00, Telefaks (+47) 71 67 83 60
ISBN nr. 82 90823 57 6
E-mail address: komf@online.no
www.kom-forlag.no

Project leader: Svein Gran
English tansalation: Text – V.F. Stokke. Recipes – Melody Favish
Graphic design: Lillyputt Grafisk Design/Kanon Grafisk Design
Graphic total production: PDC Tangen 2000

Stein MORTENSEN Morten SCHAKENDA Charles TJESSEM Per EIDE

A Plateful of SHELLS

Kom Forlag

NORWEGIAN SHELLFISH
delicacies from our coastal treasury

The sea is a valuable resource, from the beach pebbles to the ocean depths. A generous fertile nature, filled with raw materials which can make our diet more exciting, healthy and varied. If we find ourselves in the right place at the right time, we can gather a variety of wild mollusks. If we do not want to or cannot gather them ourselves, we can buy them at a fish market or order them from our local shop. All shellfish sold in Norway are farmed in clean water and controlled before they reach the public.

You can combine shellfish with fish you have caught yourself or bought in the market, and you can serve them with other products of the sea, such as crabs and shrimp. The possibilities are endless. Fresh seafood can be a real culinary experience. The most delicious seafood dishes can be the easiest to prepare. Dishes made with shellfish also can be world class cuisine. Terje Ness took the gold at "Bocuse d'Or", the unofficial world championships for chefs, with a dish that featured Norwegian scallops.

Fresh shellfish is becoming easier to obtain. Norway has an unbelievably long coastline and lots of clean water. Many areas are well-suited to shellfish farming, and its potential is far from being reached. Shellfish farming increases gradually along the coast. There is production of common mussels, oysters and scallops. In addition, systematic harvesting and processing of wild shellfish are being organized. Divers harvest horse mussels and scallops, and people along the coast are learning how to gather cockles and clams during low tide. What was once discarded or used as bait has become a valuable secondary catch and new resources, healthy, delicious and safe food. With supplies from shellfish farmers and shellfish harvesters, the processing plants are able to sell many different products: common mussels, King scallops, Iceland scallops, oysters, cockles, horse mussels, clams, and other seafood,

It is not just about flavor, but also about esthetics and love of food. Shellfish are beautiful, symmetrical, fascinating wonders. They are both food and decoration. The dishes should be just as beautiful as the ingredients themselves.

9

such as sea urchins, sea snails, crabs and seaweed. Availability to consumers varies, but that is also connected with demand. The more often customers ask for shellfish, the more likely that fish markets and shops will sell them.

Most shellfish is sold fresh, but companies are working with alternatives. Studies are being made of product life span and quality after heat treatment, cooking, freezing and canning. Eventually, bivalves will find their way into the world of ready-meals, and that is a positive development. Certainly, many exciting products will appear on the market, but they will never be able to compete with fresh bivalves. Use fresh whenever possible.

Shellfish are resource-friendly food

Bivalves live by filtering food from water they draw in through their shells. They catch microscopic algae, bacteria and tiny organic particles, guiding them in a stream along their gills and into their mouths. This food represents what we call "primary production" – the first step in the oceanic food chain. Microscopic algae grow by using nutrients found in seawater, car-

bon dioxide and energy from the sun – the same way plants grow on land. Bacteria survive by breaking down simple molecules found in water – as in soil on land. By eating shellfish, we are harvesting the products of the sea in the most resource-friendly matter, without wasting energy by going further up the food chain – to fish and animals. A ton of algae can produce as much as a hundred kilos (220 lb) of bivales. Used as fish fodder, that same ton produces only around ten kilos (22 lb) of fish. If the fish is used as pig fodder, then we end up with only one kilo (2 1/4 lb) of meat. That's only a couple of chops, after skin, bone and offal are discarded.

Products of time and place

Shellfish are healthy – on the whole. They are a good source of protein, contain marine fatty acids and many important vitamins, as well as an excellent source of iodine and other trace elements. But, if they grow in polluted waters, they can absorb substances which are bad for us, such as heavy metals and many kinds of organic pollution. The principle is the same

whether they absorb good or bad substances. It is important that shellfish are cultivated in and harvested from clean, unpolluted places. Both shellfish and locations where they are harvested have to be monitored and controlled in a responsible manner.

Shellfish are products of the water they live and grow in – both positively and negatively. The quality varies according to the area of cultivation, the season and the handling they receive after they are taken from the water. This is not surprising, as it is much the same with other products. There is a season for almost everything, and we all know of regions which produce something better or different from other places. In Norway, we consider Lofoten cod especially good, and Hardanger apples are unique. The people of Bergen swear by strawberries from Askøy, and wine lovers know that the Chardonnay grape is best in Burgundy. At the same time, we know that bad treatment can transform an excellent product into a total disaster. Shellfish are living creatures that need suitable growing areas and proper handling. They are fresh products which must be handled accordingly – from the time they are harvested until they appear on our plates.

Freshness and poison

Shellfish get their flavor from the algae they have digested, their saltiness from the water they live in, and their sweetness from the amount of nutrients they have been able to store. In addition, they will always contain a number of natural substances found in seawater. All of these factors work together to create them.

But there is also a negative side to this ability to absorb substances from seawater. They can, at times, become poisonous. Most people know about this problem, and many have probably heard old wives' tales: harvest only from places where there is a current,

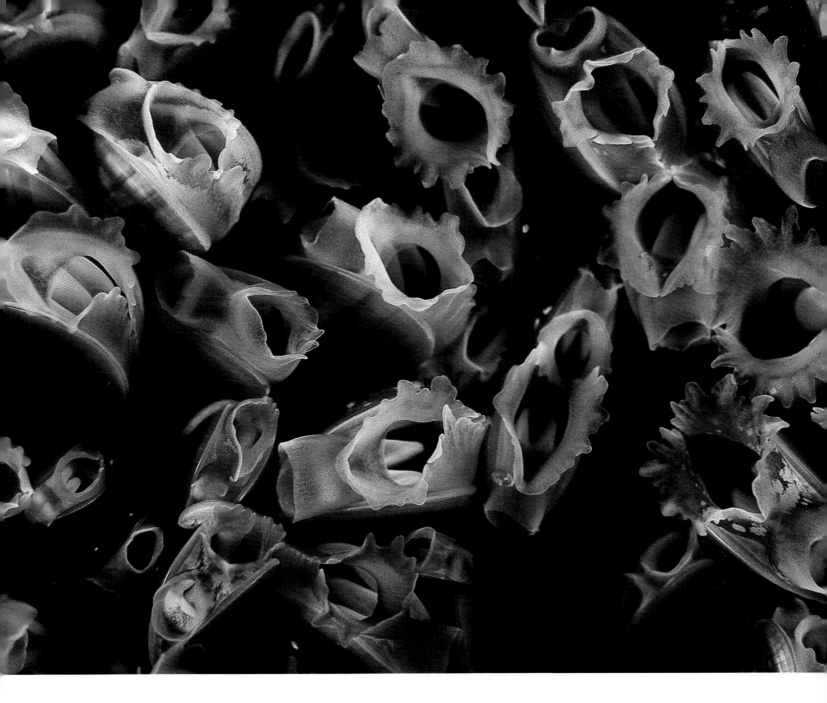

then they are edible; if you place a silver spoon in the pot and it doesn't turn black, they are edible; if you soak them in deep water for two days, they lose their poison, etc. Forget all you've heard. It is all wrong. Algae are plants and some plants are poisonous, both on land and at sea. In principle, there is little difference between land and sea, and absolutely nothing mystical about it. While a carrot is one of the healthiest roots we can eat, the root of the water hemlock is lethal. When animals and plants eat non-poisonous algae, they produce healthy material. When they ingest poisonous algae, they be-

come poisonous, and they remain poisonous until they have consumed enough "good" algae to overpower the toxins. How fast this happens depends upon several factors, and there is no fast rule.

Algae poisoning - not a new phenomenon

Algae poisoning is not a new problem. Algae have "always" been around. This increased focus on poisonous shellfish is probably a result of more frequent inspections. There are thousands of types of algae in the sea, and which one is the most dominant depends

The mussels have turned in the direction of the water current. They draw in water through an opening in the mantle, and with it come particles of food - microscopic algae, bacteria and other tiny organic particles. The primary production of the sea becomes delicate bivalve meat.

upon many factors, including the amount of nutrients in the sea, temperature, sunlight and salinity of the water. The changes occurring within the algae population are natural, regular and more or less predictable.

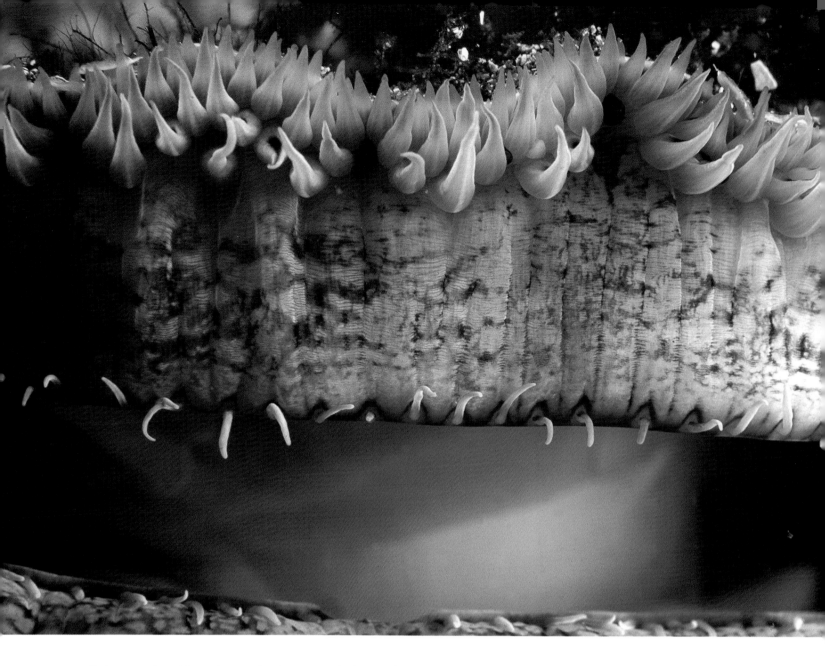

Poisonous algae bloom in certain places and at certain times, and this creates problems, in some places more frequently, in other places less often. We have to be especially watchful in the spring and late summer, and in some places, it looks like the problems are more serious farther into the fjords than out by the coast.

There are two main groups of toxins which cause problems. The one group is called DSP (diarrhetic shellfish poison) and causes unpleasant but harmless diarrhea. The other is PSP (paralytic shellfish poison) and can cause nerve paralysis which can be life-threatening in extreme cases. These toxins are colorless, tasteless, and odorless and remain in the shellfish even after they have been dried and/or cooked. It is obvious why shellfish must be controlled before we use them!

Inspection of shellfish

Since shellfish also can ingest and store other unpleasant substances, not just algae, we also have to consider ocean pollution. Shellfish must be harvested from areas which are a safe distance from sewers and other potentially negative runoff. Shellfish producers have learned to understand the differences in time and geography, and they farm shellfish only in areas which are clean, and they harvest them only during

The scallop has opened - to sense the world around it on the bottom of the sea. Numerous tentacles, richly endowed with sensing cells, "taste" the water - searching for food or the aroma of other mollusks - or maybe that of a predator. Small eyes lie like pearls along the mantle between the tentacles. The scallop can distinguish light and shade and feel movement.

periods known to be safe. But each shipment of shellfish which is going to be sold still has to be inspected. All shellfish on the Norwegian market are safe for the consumer, free from algae toxins, harmful bacteria and pollution.

Harvesting shellfish on your own

Of course, the shells we harvest on our own have to be clean and free of toxins and harmful microbes, but it is too expensive for individuals to send their harvest for control. If you live along the Norwegian coast, there may be a monitoring station near you, and thus current information about the algae situation in your area. No monitoring system is full-proof, because the stations are usually relatively far apart and algae growth can be confined to a small area. So gathering edible bivalves is always done at your own risk, but the risk can be minimized with some simple knowledge. It is not that complicated:

1: Ask for available information and updates from the monitoring station nearest you. If you harvest nearby, you can feel safe. If the whole coast is problem-free, you are probably on the safe side, even if you harvest other places. If you are far from a monitoring station, be careful. Remember, you can always buy controlled shellfish at your local fish market.

2. There are differences among bivalve species. Exercise the most caution with mussels. They live where there is most likely dense algae concentration, and they seem to filter algae more effectively than other bivalves. They grow quickly, but they also become poisonous faster than other species. Scallops are the safest. They are almost never poisonous, for two reasons. First, they live under the level of water with highest algae concentration, so they are not so exposed to toxic algae as shells in shallower water. Second, most toxins are concentrated in the digestive system, and we do not eat that part of the scallop.

3. Harvest from clean waters. As mentioned earlier, shellfish are filter-feeders and ingest whatever particles happen to be in the water around them. We can become ill from eating raw or lightly-cooked shellfish which contain bacteria from fertilizer or sewage. Shellfish which grow close to built-up areas or harbours can ingest small amounts of gasoline or diesel fuel present in the water. It does not take much to make it taste bad. Shellfish which grow in polluted water are polluted themselves. It is as simple as that.

Are you allergic?

Use common sense when eating shellfish. Many foods contain substances that can cause allergic reactions, and unfortunately, many people are allergic to shellfish such as shrimp, crab, lobster and bivalves. Food allergies are a problem that we have to live with. It is very important to know one's own reactions. People with other allergies should be careful when testing their limits – do not overdo shellfish consumption just because you think everything will be all right. Really, everyone should limit their intake of shellfish. Everything in moderation – even delicacies.

MUSSELS

tasty weeds

Mussels can be found almost everywhere along the coast. In the spring, when algae bloom and the water temperature rises to 8-10°C (45-50°F), they spawn in synchrony. When one starts, the others follow. Soon, the water is brimming with eggs and sperm. When the eggs are fertilized, they turn into larvae about a tenth of a millimeter long. These larvae swarm in the water for a few weeks, grazing on microscopic, planctonic algae. When they settle down on a hard surface and turn into spat, the world seems full of mussel spat. Everywhere, on buoys, rocks, quays and boat hulls, the mussels grow like weeds – tasty weeds.

The majority of spring mussels do not live to maturity – they are crushed, crowded out, eaten by fish, crabs, and birds. Many fish and animals gorge on mussel spat. But many still survive. If they get enough nourishment, they become heavy and meaty. If they live too close together or in a place with few nutrients, they are thin and uninteresting. If they are harvested from a sandy bottom, they are often full of sand and pearls. Find your own mussel bed – harvest the overflow of good, meaty shells and enjoy them when they are best, before spawning in the spring, or during the fall and winter, when they have grown plump again. There is nothing like a big pot of steamed mussels. It smells of the sea and you can almost hear the waves.

Mussel cultivation

Mussel farmers use nature's own overflow of larvae. When the larvae swarm, the farmers hang ropes in the sea at places with the densest concentration of larvae. When their period as plankton is over, the larvae attach themselves to the ropes. The principle for producing mussels is simple. After they have attached themselves to the rope, they remain in the sea until they are ready to be harvested. But there

Although tightly squeezed and ingrown, mussels are still able to stretch themselves up to oxygen and nutrient-rich water. Creatures on the sea floor compete for both space and food.

net tubes or "stockings". The mussels attach themselves, turn toward the best access to food and water, and they grow gradually out of the stocking. After a while, the stocking looks like a thick sausage filled with mussels facing out toward the water.

In the best areas, it is possible to harvest small but meaty mussels after about a year – before they spawn for the first time. Usually, the mussels are left to hang for a season or two before they are harvested. At harvest time, many tons are removed from the sea. This is heavy work when done by hand. Today, most harvesting and processing is done with special boats and equipment. The mussels pass through a production line where bunches of mussels are picked off the ropes, separated, cleaned, inspected, sorted and packaged before they are

ready to be sold. Effective, modern production, harvest and transportation makes it possible to have year-round access to clean, plump, toxin-free mussels. This gives us a long mussel season.

Almost all mussels sold in Norway are farmed. The production is a little different in Rissa, at Fosen in Trøndelag. For years, mussels have been harvested from rich stocks in a tidal current with a grab which is steered from a flat-bottomed barge. This is one example that emphasizes

Lysefjorden Shell, Norway's largest mussel farm, is based in Lysefjord, Rogaland, with the mighty rock formation "Pulpit Rock" in the background. Row after row of gray buoys blend in with the color of the terrain and support a plant which hides tons of mussels under the surface of the water.

are many means to an end, with a number of challenges along the way. Mussel farmers are preparing a strategy for continued harvesting. The rope can be left hanging where it is, or it can be moved to other places where the mussels can grow until they are harvested. They are often thinned out, so that their numbers do not become too overwhelming as they grow. One widely used method is to gather small shells from the ropes and fill them into

how important it is to harmonize mussel production with nature; to find the right time, place, and strategy. The perfect density of larvae, enough food, good growth, the least amount of toxic algae, no eider ducks and good geographical placement which makes the rest of the process as practical as possible. When the mussels are ready to be harvested, the rest is simply "technique and business".

Mussels in the kitchen

Fresh mussels must be alive. Live mussels are supposed to be closed, so if some shells are partly open, they may be dead, so tap them against the countertop. If they are alive, they will close. Mussels are best and easiest to use if they are cleaned before preparation. Shells you pick yourself often are covered in algae and have thick beards, while farmed mussels are usually cleaner and more "ready to use". If the mussels stick together in a bunch, they should be separated. Remove beards and scrub clean, but do not overdo it. The most important thing is to remove the beards and any mud on the shells.

Everything inside a mussel is edible. Mussels have their own distinctive flavor, unlike any other seafood, and they can be used in many ways – in

A mussel colony is a complete society in miniature. On and in between the shells are algae and animals such as barnacles, sponges, brushworms and sea anemones. Some are visible, some are not.

fish and shellfish soups and as an ingredient in combination with other shellfish and fish. The possibilities are endless. Enjoy on different occasions. They are just as good when prepared simply, steamed in their own stock, as they are in more complicated dishes on a festive table. We have chosen a number of recipes which illustrate a range of possibilities.

Choice of beverage depends greatly on how the mussels are prepared. For steamed mussels, and dishes in which the mussel's own distinctive flavor is most important, it is best to focus on the freshness of the food and at the same time create a little contrast to the clean, salty as well as sweet, robust mussel flavor. For steamed mussels, white bread and lemon, mineral water with lemon or lime is a perfect thirst quencher, and it does not drown out the flavor of the mussels. Cold light beer or a light Pilsner is also a good accompaniment, if the occasion suits. Or choose a dry, young white wine with a little body and freshness – a Viño verde, Muscadet – as young as possible, maybe a Riesling from Alsace, a Sauvignon blanc – maybe from New Zealand, or a dry, fresh Italian. If the mussels or mussel dish is spicy, then it is important to serve a wine with enough body. Many mussel dishes use a cream-based stock or a relatively rich sauce. This will overpower many dry white wines. The richness of the stock and sauce has to harmonize with the body of the wine. Chardonnay wines are usually excellent choices. Wines based on Pinot Gris or Sauvignon blanc and many ordinary Spanish white wines are also suitable. Some Spanish wines are treated as "reserva-wines" and have been aged in oak barrels. This gives them an especially strong flavor – challenging, exciting and demanding when served with rich mussel dishes – but have an alternative waiting, just in case your guests are not ready for your interesting choice.

MUSSELS ON THE FIRE

Few things taste better than what you have gathered yourself – whether it is wild berries from the forest or mussels found among the rocks near the shore. Here are two ideas for preparing them, the first from Sunnmøre on the west coast of Norway and then a French variation with roots in Brittany.

1: Gather as many mussels as you need for generous servings. Find a natural indentation in a large boulder and fill it with dry grass, heather and a few splinters of driftwood. Top with mussels and light with a match. When the fire has died down, pick hot mussels right out of the coals and eat just as they are, hot and lightly smoked. Serve with fresh bread, butter and mayonnaise.

2: Give all guests or participants in the dinner a glass of good wine each, and make them work making a so-called "eclade". Arrange mussels in a large rosette on a hard surface on the ground. Sprinkle with a layer of pine needles and light with a match. Sprinkle with extra needles to make sure mussels cook evenly. When the fire has died down, pick hot mussels right out of the coals.

MUSSELS STEAMED IN WHITE WINE

2 kg (4 1/2 lb) mussels
2 shallots
1 garlic clove
2 tablespoons olive oil
1 tablespoon unsalted butter
1 dl (1/2 cup) white wine
1 tablespoon chopped parsley

Steaming is an easy, tasty and popular way to prepare mussels. There are countless flavorings you can add. Here is a classic dish:

Place mussels in cold running water for 15-20 minutes. Scrub and rinse well. Clean and mince shallot and garlic and sauté in oil in a saucepan. Add mussels, butter and white wine, cover and steam until all have opened. Remove mussels and keep warm. Reduce liquid until 1/3 of the original amount remains. Pour over mussels. Sprinkle with parsley and serve with hearty bread.

STEAMED MUSSELS WITH FENNEL AND CURRY

2 kg (4 1/2 lb) mussels
2 shallots
1 fennel
1/2 leek
1 tablespoon red curry paste
1 tablespoon butter
1/2 dl (3 1/2 tablespoons) white wine
2 dl (1 cup) whipping cream
2 tablespoons butter
juice and grated zest of 1 lime
fresh coriander and other fresh herbs

Place mussels in cold, running water for 15-20 minutes. Scrub and rinse well. Clean and chop shallot, thinly slice fennel and leek. Sauté vegetables with curry paste in butter in a heavy saucepan. Add wine and reduce until 1/3 of the original amount remains. Add mussels, cover and steam until all have opened.

Strain stock, add cream and bring to a boil. Add butter and mix with an immersion blender until frothy. Stir in lime juice, zest and coriander. Divide mussels and vegetables among four deep soup bowls and pour over hot sauce. Serve with hearty bread.

BEVERAGE SUGGESTION

Red curry and fennel add a strong, sharp flavor. Serve with beer or white wine with some sweetness to balance the strength of the dish.

Steamed mussels with fennel and curry.

STEAMED MUSSELS WITH CURRY AND COCONUT

2 kg (4 1/2 lb) mussels
1/2 onion
1 garlic clove
2 tablespoons curry paste
1 tablespoon olive oil
1 dl (1/2 cup) white wine
2 dl (1 cup) coconut milk
(do not use coconut cream)
1 tablespoon chopped coriander

Place mussels in cold running water for 15-20 minutes. Scrub and rinse well. Clean and chop onion and garlic. Sauté vegetables with curry paste in olive oil in a heavy pot. Add wine and reduce until 1/3 of the original amount remains. Add mussels, cover and steam until all have opened. Add coconut milk and simmer 3 minutes. Mussels should not cook more than 5-6 minutes total. Sprinkle with coriander.

BEVERAGE SUGGESTION

Serve with a dry or semi-dry white wine. Green tea or light beer also work well with this dish.

If you need more ways to make steamed mussels, here are a couple of good altenatives:

Mussels with tomatoes and chile:
Steam mussels with ripe tomatoes, garlic, shallots, chile pepper and dried tomatoes,

Mussels with curry and spring onions:
Steam mussels with curry, shallot, spring onion, cayenne and white wine.

LENTIL SOUP WITH CRISPY MUSSELS

Mussels

1 kg (2 1/4 lb) mussels
1/2 loaf white bread
1/2 garlic clove
1 tablespoon chopped chives
1 tablespoon chopped parsley
8 satay sticks
4 tablespoons (1/4 cup)
all-purpose flour
1 egg, lightly beaten
4 tablespoons (1/4 cup) oil

Place mussels in cold running water for 15-20 minutes. Scrub and rinse well. Place in a dry hot pan, cover and steam until all have opened. Strain stock to use in soup. Remove from shells. Thread 5-6 mussels onto each satay stick. Add remaining mussels to soup at serving time.

Make crumbs with bread, garlic and herbs and pour onto a plate. Dip mussel sticks first in flour (shake off excess flour), then in egg and last in breadcrumbs. Place on paper towels and refrigerate until ready to fry.

Soup

6 tablespoons green lentils
1 garlic clove
1 shallot
3/4 dl (1/3 cup) diced onion
1/2 dl (3 1/2 tablespoons) diced carrot
1 1/4 dl (1/2 cup) diced potato
7 1/2 dl (3 cups) full-fat milk
4 dl (1 2/3 cup) mild mussel stock
salt and pepper
fresh chervil

Soak lentils in water for about 2 hours. Cook vegetables in milk and stock until tender. Mash and strain or serve soup as it is. Season with salt and pepper.

Just before serving, fry mussel sticks in oil until crisp. Arrange remaining mussels in four deep bowls. Bring soup to a boil and mix with an immersion blender until frothy. Garnish with chervil.

PESTO-MARINATED MUSSELS ON TOAST

1 kg (2 1/4 lb) mussels
1/2 dl (3 1/2 tablespoons) olive oil
1/2 dl (3 1/2 tablespoons) white wine
2 shallots
1 garlic clove

Place mussels in cold running water for 15-20 minutes. Scrub and rinse well. Clean and chop shallots and garlic. Sauté in oil in a saucepan. Add mussels and white wine, cover and steam until all have opened. Cool, then remove from shells.

PESTO (made according to
basic recipe page 109)

Combine pesto and mussels. Season with salt and pepper, if desired.

1/2 loaf white bread
1 dl (scant 1/2 cup) olive oil
1 garlic clove
salt

Thinly slice bread and remove crust. Fry in oil with garlic and a little salt until crisp on both sides. Top with pesto-marinated mussels. You can also serve these mussels in hollowed-out tomatoes. Scald and peel tomatoes. Halve and remove seeds. Fill with marinated mussels.

23

MUSSELS AU GRATIN

2 kg (4 1/2) mussels
coarse sea salt
2 large garlic cloves, minced
2 tablespoons chopped flat-leaf
parsley
grated zest of 1 lemon
breadcrumbs with herbs
(see page 109, use 1/2 amount)
3 tablespoons unsalted butter
1 lemon, in wedges

Clean and steam mussels as described on page 17. Remove top shells, leaving mussels in bottom shells.

Preheat oven to 250ºC (475ºF) or preheat grill. Cover bottom of an oven-proof dish with salt. Place mussels on salt and sprinkle with garlic, parsley, lemon zest and crumbs. Place a dot of butter on each mussel. Bake 10 minutes. Serve with bread and lemon.

SCALLOPS
jewels of the sea

Hand-picked delicacies

The great ocean beds are the treasure chests of the coast. We can harvest valuable products all the way from the sandy beach to the lower depths. Mollusks, flat fish, crabs – and down in the depths, Norway lobsters and shrimp. The scallop is perhaps the finest jewel of them all – one of the finest ingredients we can harvest from the sea.

At the same time, the scallop is an exciting and different mollusk. While the oyster sits silent, blind and immobile from the moment the larva chooses a suitable spot, and the common mussel can only move around a little with its foot and byssus, the scallop has an unusual life, compared with the other bivalves. It lies freely on the ocean floor, either completely or partially buried in the sediment. By clapping their shells together and pressing water through their mantle, scallops can swim. They can jump along the seabed, forward, backward, rotate, rock themselves down into the sand and camouflage themselves to escape an enemy. Scallops can make decisions. And, they can see. They have a row of small eyes on the edge of the mantle, between the tentacles, which help them feel things. These eyes are surprisingly like our own, just of a simpler design. Scallops do not have sharp eyesight, but they can see light, shadow and movement.

Scallops are relatively rare along the southern Norwegian coast, but rich fields can be found along the northwestern Norwegian coast and in Trøndelag. The northernmost stocks are in Nordland. Scallops thrive best on the ocean bed with sand, mud and fine gravel, usually at 10 to 30 meters depth. Sometimes they can be found in even shallower water, and those which are found in deeper water are not so familiar to us. That means that scallops live within diving depth, and Norwegian scallops are harvested by divers. They are hand-picked, sorted

Hand-picked delicacies - scallops from one of the rich stocks along the coast. Divers with a little bit of practice can land large catches, and harvested with restraint, these mollusks are a valuable and renewable resource which can be tapped without any interference in nature.

The scallop is lying visible on top of the sand. It stretches its tentacles, senses and gets ready to escape - from the diver, a starfish, or maybe a crab.

according to size, cleaned of sand, whole and undamaged. Norwegian scallops are perfect. In most other places, scallops are harvested with special trawlers or shellfish scrapers. There is limited use for such scallop-harvesting machinery in Norway, because the seabed is too irregular and the harvesters can get stuck easily. Another problem is that scrapers may destroy the seabed. They sometimes rip up the entire bed, collecting everything that grows there, crushing shells, ripping and battering other creatures who live there, and they

destroy the living conditions – a not very environmentally-friendly method of collection, which is incompatible with our desire to preserve nature.

Scallops are not just harvested by professionals. They are a great catch for amateur divers – one of the best things the sea has to offer. The joy and enthusiasm of finding an area filled with large scallops is something every diver hopes to experience – now and forever. We feel rich when we bring our catch home and invite friends over to enjoy them. But as mentioned earlier, scallop stocks in some areas are threatened by plundering. We are worried, as are the shellfish companies, and many others. A few can ruin it for everyone else. We can cooperate to remove the problem.

Scallop farming, the exciting creation of a new industry

The dream of cultivating the sea is an old one. All over the world, innumerable fish species, mollusks, snails, crayfish, sea urchins and sea cucumbers have been "caged". Norway has domesticated the salmon. We have mastered cod and turbot farming, and we are working hard to get halibut production to an industrial level. Mussels and oysters have been farmed for a long time. And now comes the scallop. The idea of farming scallops is inviting, given its huge international market, high status and high price. With good biological ballast and some knowledge about scallop farming in China and Japan, the University of Bergen set about trying to farm our largest species of scallop – *Pecten maximus* – under controlled conditions.

They had contact with researchers in Brest, France, where they were in the process of producing spat for restocking the scallop fields.

Eventually, the University of Bergen, the Institute of Marine Research and Hordaland county council joined together to form the Norwegian Scallop Program in 1994. The program was supported by the coastal counties, and slowly there developed a network of producers who wanted to try scallop farming. Hordaland county helped to coordinate this endeavor. Researchers at the Institute of Marine Research gave advice and coordinated research activity on the scallop. A number of experimental projects were initiated, and soon, Norway's top minds were working toward the same goal: scallop farming in Norway. The connection between research and business was close, and very special. During a time when shellfish producers had no interest organization of their own, the Scallop Program became a safe "umbrella" for them.

The Scallop Program eventually gathered together not just scallop

The shell jumps up from a cloud of sand along the bottom for a short distance, before it settles down once again.

farmers, but also those interested in farming mussels, as well as those who wanted to increase oyster production in Norway. At the end of 1998, the Scallop Program was near its end, and the business side of the venture was at a turning point. Shellfish farming had been reestablished and organized in Norway. It had taken a few hectic years, but the farming of scallops, had we really managed to do that? Well, it can take time to domesticate a new species. Not enough time has passed from 1994 to today for us to have solved all the problems associated with large-scale farming. But from two single scallops at the University of Bergen in 1985, we have developed a production of spat in a hatchery which produces several million scallop spat per year. Experimental farming of scallop spat which were hung in baskets along the coast has taught us about the correct conditions for small scallops, and the results of placement of half-grown scallops on the ocean floor are beginning to teach us what works and what does not. We are part of the way, but we have not reached our goal yet. For those of us who celebrate every time we can put scallops on the table, we hope to reach that goal, with first-class scallops, always available, as the result.

Choose large scallops, before they spawn

Scallops are harvested when they have grown to at least 10 cm (4"). Then they are four or five years old. The age can be deciphered on the shell, as with the yearly rings of a tree. When the scallop has enough food and suitable growing conditions, it makes a new calcium ring at the shell edge every day. Growth slows down during the fall, as the temperature falls. The growth rings become closer and closer together and then cease forming over the winter. In the spring, the scallop begins to grow again, and during that

time, a light ring forms on the shell. During its first winter, the scallop is the size of a fingernail, so its first ring can be hard to see and just has to be calculated into its age. When the scallop is more than six or seven, growth rate decreases and it begins to drop in weight. We are particularly interested in the relationship between the weight of the shell and the weight of the edible parts. Whether we dive for scallops or buy them at the fish market, we want a large, white muscle in each. As a scallop grows from ten to twelve centimeters (4-5"), the muscle grows even more. Sometimes the scallop can almost double in weight during this period, from four and a half to five or six years of age. That means that we get the most food from each scallop if the shell has been allowed to grow to twelve centimeters.

Scallops are hermaphrodites – both male and female at the same time. In mature scallops, it is easy to see the division between the light male part and the red-orange female part. The "coral" is beautiful and full of flavor. Just as it is important to choose scallops with a large muscle, it is also a good idea to eat them before they spawn, when the coral is full. Spawning takes place in the summer. Examinations of maturation rates in Norwegian scallops indicate that there are some differences in the different stocks living in different places along the coast. While scallops in Hordaland spawn throughout the summer, spawning in Trøndelag is more synchronized over a short period of time in midsummer. These observations are interesting and show that the scallops have adapted spawning strategy to living conditions.

A third important thing to consider is that the scallop's large muscle is not just used for opening, closing and swimming. It is also a storehouse of energy. Much of the scallop's energy reserves, which include glycogen, are stored in that large muscle. When it is

Usually, the large white muscle and coral (roe and milt) are the only parts of a scallop which are used.

in good condition, the muscle is large, firm, springy – and sweet. The better the conditions for growth, the more nourishment stored in the muscle. The strategy of all shellfish is to be in the best condition for spawning, so that when they produce roe and sperm, they expend all the energy they can afford. Much of the sweetness in the muscle disappears, and it is not so firm and springy. The muscles are not much to brag about during this period.

The result of the scallop's natural life cycle is that the quality of both muscle and coral – and the relationship between the two – vary with the seasons. The coral is plump and well-developed just before spawning, while the sweetness of the muscle disappears. During and after spawning, no shells are particularly interesting. As they build themselves up again over the autumn, the quality of the large white muscle improves, and gradually the coral develops as well. As mentioned, there are local variations, but during the late winter and spring, we can get scallops with both good coral and large sweet muscles.

Opening and serving scallops

Usually scallops are opened and cleaned before use. Hold the scallop deep side down. Guide a sharp, short and thin-bladed knife in between the two shells, on the side where the large white muscle sits, as indicated in the illustration, closely along the inner edge of the flat shell. When the muscle

is cut loose from the shell, it opens. Remove that shell. In the scallop, the different body parts are well separated and are easy to find. The large white muscle and the coral, which contains both roe and milt are the parts we use.

We can either rip out the mantle, gills and digestive gland before we cut the muscle loose from the deep shell, or we can cut the muscle loose and cut or clip away mantle, gills and digestive gland afterwards. The muscle also can be loosened from the shell with a spoon. A short kitchen scissors can be good to have for fine cleaning – but watch your fingers. When initial cleaning is finished, we have remaining white muscle and coral. They are connected if we have cleaned with a knife or scissors, or they are separate if we have removed what we don't use with our fingers. Otherwise, any more treatment depends upon how the scallop is to be used. The two flat brownish bands which lie on the white muscle are the kidneys. They can be cut away, so that the muscle is completely white and delicate.

Do not place in water, because it absorbs water and loses flavor. Rinse quickly if necessary, and drain on paper or cotton towels.

The liquid in the shells can be used as stock, as long as it is clear and pure. It has a fine fresh shellfish flavor when fresh. If the digestive gland has been punctured, it will turn brownish and

unappetizing. The shells can be used only as decoration.

Take good care of the scallop's own distinctive flavor!

Sweetness, a mild, lobster-like shellfish taste and a hint of the sea are the most characteristic flavors in a fresh scallop. In order to preserve these fine flavor elements, it is important not to overpower the scallop's own flavor. Used raw, this isn't a problem as long as we are careful with spices and garnishes. Heat-treated shells are more demanding. Do not cook, steam or sauté them for too long. Then the shellfish liquid evaporates and the muscle shrinks and becomes small, dry and uninteresting.

Frying or grilling brings out the sweetness of scallops, and that is a challenge. How to create harmony with that fresh sweetness, without overpowering it and yet allowing for some contrast? Choose a good Sancerre, a Chablis, a Burgundy or another light-bodied Chardonnay wine without too much oak dominance. Mature Rieslings from Germany or Alsace are also good alternatives. Stay away from rich Australian or American "Burgundies" and German wines with too much residual sweetness. Use the same wines as with mussels. The more natural the state of the scallop, the younger and drier the wine. The richer the sauce, the more cream, seasonings and stock in the dish, the richer, more full-bodied wine. And remember that scallops are the best and most beautiful bivalves in the sea. They are perfect for a party and deserves the best company, and your best bottle. Good luck!

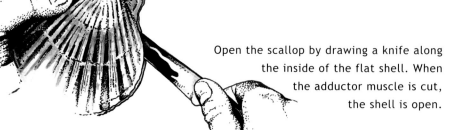

Open the scallop by drawing a knife along the inside of the flat shell. When the adductor muscle is cut, the shell is open.

DISHES WITH SCALLOPS

Scallops au gratin

This is a simple and popular way to prepare scallops. Try different versions, but do not forget two important principles: do not cook for too long and do not season too much. Here is one suggestion:

Scallops au gratin with garlic-sautéed spinach

SCALLOPS AU GRATIN WITH GARLIC-SAUTÉED SPINACH

Only the white muscle of the scallop is used in this dish.

Scallops

8 scallops
1 tablespoon olive oil
salt and pepper

Open and clean scallops. Scrape and wash four curved lower shells. Just before serving, cut each scallop into three slices and brown quickly on one side in oil, preferably in an iron or non-stick pan. Correct browning is very important to bring out the sweetness of the scallop.

Sauce

1 shallot
1 tablespoon unsalted butter
1 dl (1/2 cup) dry white wine
4 dl (1 2/3 cups) fish stock
(see page 111)
2 dl (1 cup) whipping cream
salt and pepper
2 egg yolks

Clean and mince shallot and sauté in butter. Add wine and reduce until a quarter of the original amount remains. Add stock and reduce until 2 dl (3/4 cup) remain. Add cream and reduce until 2 dl (3/4 cup) remain. Season with salt and pepper. Just before serving, whisk in egg yolks and heat carefully until mixture thickens slightly.

Garlic-sautéed spinach

200 g (7 oz) fresh spinach
1 garlic clove
salt and pepper

Clean and rinse spinach well, removing all coarse stalks. Mince garlic. Sauté spinach and garlic quickly in butter.

Preheat oven, preferably with a grill element, to 200°C (400°F). Divide spinach among the shells, top with scallops and spoon over sauce. Just before serving, place shells in oven 4-6 minutes, until golden. Serve immediately with good homemade bread.

SPICED SCALLOPS WITH CARAMELIZED ENDIVE AND LEMON-BLACK SALSIFY

Black salsify, sometimes called poor man's asparagus, is a mild-flavored vegetable, which should be used more often. You can substitute parsnips or celeriac, but the flavor will be different. Endive, also called chicory, is rather bitter, but interesting. It gets milder if placed in cold water for a while. Otherwise, you can use any other green leafy vegetable which can be cooked, such as celery cabbage.

6–8 scallops

Lemon-black salsify

4 black salsify
5 dl (2 cups) water
3 dl (1 1/4 cups) full-fat milk
1 teaspoon salt
1 tablespoon butter
2 tablespoons sugar
juice of 1 lemon
1/2 teaspoon minced fresh chile pepper

Caramelized endive

2 endives
1 tablespoon sugar
3 tablespoons butter

Spice Blend

2 teaspoons salt
1 teaspoon ground black pepper
1 teaspoon dried thyme
1/2 teaspoon ground cloves
1/2 teaspoon ground ginger
1/4 teaspoon ground cinnamon

3 tablespoons olive oil/butter
fresh coriander

Scallops

Open and clean scallops. Use only the large white muscle in this dish. (See illustration for opening and description of cleaning on page 30). Rinse scallops quickly, if necessary, and dry with paper towels. Cut in half horizontally, cover with plastic wrap and refrigerate until just before serving.

Black salsify

Peel and cut each root into three pieces of equal size. Bring water, milk and salt to a boil. Add roots and cook until almost tender, about 5 minutes. Drain and keep warm. Melt butter and sugar to a light caramel, add lemon juice and reduce slightly. Stir in chile and let simmer until tender and covered with caramel. Remove roots and keep warm. Reduce sauce to a thick syrup.

Endive

Clean endive and split horizontally. Cook in at least 1 liter (4 cups) lightly salted water until tender, 30-60 seconds. Drain on paper towels. Sprinkle with sugar and cook in butter until golden.

Combine spices and sprinkle over scallops. Sauté in oil or butter until golden. Arrange black salsify in center of plates. Place endive across roots and top with scallops. Drizzle with lemon syrup. Garnish with fresh coriander.

The large delicate white muscle of the scallop is very good served raw. Cut it into thin slices and garnish with something in a contrasting color. Or flavor it with a little olive oil, a drop of lime or lemon and a little salt and pepper. Here is a suggestion for a marinade.

RAW MARINATED SCALLOPS WITH HERB SALAD

6–8 scallops

Marinade

1 shallot
1/2 garlic clove
1/8 red chile pepper
grated zest and juice of 1 lime
1/2 (3 1/2 tablespoons) extra virgin olive oil
1 tablespoon walnut oil
salt and pepper
fresh coriander

fresh herbs (dill, flat-leaf parsley, basil and coriander) assorted salad greens (lollo, arugula, red lettuce)

Scallops

Open and clean scallops. Use only the large white muscle in this dish. (See illustration for opening and description of cleaning on page 30). Rinse scallops quickly, if necessary, and dry with paper towels. Cover with plastic and refrigerate until just before serving.

Marinade

Clean and mince shallot and garlic and place in a small bowl. Split chile, remove ribs and seeds and mince. Add with lime zest. Whisk in lime juice and both oils. Season with salt, pepper and coriander.

Salad

Clean and rinse salad greens and place in cold water to make them crisp. Drain and dry with paper towels so dressing sticks to greens and herbs.

Thinly slice scallops and arrange in a ring on each plate. Brush with marinade. Fold remaining marinade into salad greens and arrange in center of each plate. Grind black pepper over scallops just before serving.

STEAMED SCALLOPS WITH WHITE WINE CREAM SAUCE AND BROCCOLI

Steaming is a gentle method of preparation which preserves the scallop's own character. Be careful in preparing and in adding seasonings and garnish.

6 scallops
1 shallot
1 tablespoon butter
1 dl (1/2 cup) white wine
1 dl (1/2 cup) water
1 dl (1/2 cup) whipping cream
salt and pepper
a few drops lime juice
1 teaspoon finely chopped chives

1 broccoli stalk
1/2 garlic clove
1 shallot
1/8 red chile pepper
1 tablespoon butter
salt and pepper

Use both muscle and coral in this dish. Clean shells and cover scallops with plastic. Refrigerate.

Clean and chop shallot. Sauté in butter. Add white wine and reduce until half the original amount remains. Add water and scallops and cover. Simmer carefully over low heat for 2-3 minutes. Remove scallops and keep warm. Increase heat, add cream and reduce by half. Season with salt, pepper, lime juice and chives.

Broccoli

Clean and cut broccoli into florets. Cook in lightly salted water about 1 minute. Plunge into cold water to cool. Drain on paper towels. Clean and mince garlic, shallot and chile and sauté in butter. Add broccoli and stir-fry 2-3 minutes. Season with salt and pepper.

Cut each scallop into two or three slices and arrange with coral, sauce and broccoli. Garnish with chives.

SAUTÉED SCALLOPS WITH PASTA, SUN-DRIED TOMATOES AND SAGE

375 g (13-14 oz) fresh pasta (see basic recipes page 108 or use ready-made pasta)
1/2 dl (3 1/2 tablespoons) extra virgin olive oil
30 g (1 oz) sun-dried tomatoes in oil, drained and chopped
1 teaspoon finely chopped fresh sage
salt and pepper

8 scallops
salt and pepper
oil

Cook fresh pasta about 3 minutes. Stir in oil, tomatoes and sage. Mix well and season with salt and pepper. Open and clean scallops. Sprinkle with salt and pepper and sauté in oil. Use cooking juices as sauce. Combine all ingredients and serve immediately.

Grilled scallops

Scallops are also good grilled. Just do not grill them for too long. The simplest way to prepare them is to grill them with oil, salt and pepper and serve with a little olive oil, chives and herbs. Here is another exciting alternative, pepper-grilled with bulgur salad. Bulgur, cracked wheat, comes from Turkey and is an unusual and exciting garnish for scallops.

PEPPER-GRILLED SCALLOPS WITH BULGUR SALAD AND ORANGE SAUCE

2 tablespoons black peppercorns

Bulgur salad

1 1/2 dl (3/4 cup) water
1 dl (1/2 cup) bulgur
salt
2 tablespoons tomato concassé (see page 109)
2 tablespoons chopped fresh herbs (chervil, tarragon, coriander, thyme)
1 tablespoon chopped shallot
1 tablespoon fresh lime juice
extra virgin olive oil
salt and pepper

Orange sauce

2 tablespoons sugar
2 dl (3/4 cup) fresh orange juice
2 tablespoons butter

4 scallops
oil

Place a frying pan over highest heat. When pan is very hot, add pepper and cook until the peppercorns "hop" – then they take on a very special flavor. Cool, then crush them in a mortar.

Bring water to a boil. Add bulgur and cover. Remove from heat and let bulgur swell for about 15 minutes. Stir in remaining ingredients.

Melt sugar in a heavy saucepan. Add orange juice and cook until about 1/2 dl (3 1/2 tablespoons) remain. Remove from heat and beat in butter. Keep sauce warm, but do not allow to boil.

Clean scallops. Brush with oil and sprinkle with pepper. Sauté quickly in oil, about 1 minute per side.

Pack bulgur salad into four low, wide cups. Unmold on plates and top with scallops. Spoon sauce all around. Garnish with fresh herbs.

SCALLOP TEMPURA WITH TERIYAKI SAUCE AND MANGOLD

This dish is Japanese-inspired. The scallops are dipped in tempura batter and deep-fried, flavored with a kind of teriyaki sauce and served with mangold. Spinach or celery cabbage can be used instead of mangold.

Tempura batter

4 tablespoons (1/4 cup) cornstarch
250 g (1 3/4 cups) all-purpose flour
1 teaspoon active dry yeast
1 teaspoon salt
4 dl (1 2/3 cups) water
2 egg whites

Place dry ingredients in a food processor. With motor running, add water and process until smooth. Strain. Beat egg whites until stiff and fold into flour mixture. Let batter rest 1-2 hours in the refrigerator.

Teriyaki sauce

1 tablespoon chopped shallot
1 tablespoon chopped fresh ginger
1 large garlic clove, chopped
3 tablespoons olive oil
1/2 dl (3 1/2 tablespoons) white wine
3 tablespoons lemon juice
1 tablespoon sugar
1 dl (scant 1/2 cup) soy sauce

Sauté shallot, ginger and garlic in oil. Add wine, juice and sugar and simmer until thick as porridge. Add soy sauce and puree in a food processor or with an immersion blender until smooth. Strain.

8 scallops
4 satay sticks
corn oil

Clean scallops. Dry well with paper towels. Thread onto sticks. Heat oil to 170°C (350°F). Deep-fry until golden, 1-2 minutes.

1 mangold
1 tablespoon chopped fresh ginger
2 garlic cloves, chopped
1 teaspoon minced chile pepper
1/2 dl (3 1/2 tablespoons) olive oil
sea salt

Chop mangold. Sauté ginger, garlic and chile in oil about 20 seconds. Add mangold and sauté until it wilts.

Arrange mounds of mangold on plates and sprinkle with sea salt. Top with scallop sticks and drizzle sauce all around.

OYSTERS
the best "fast food" in the world

Open and eat! A fresh, beautiful and healthy eating experience in under 15 seconds. In every corner of the world, they have caught on to this one. More than a million tons of oysters per year is no joke. This is large-scale food production. If we sum up oyster production in China, Korea, Japan, the US and France, we get just about one million tons. The better part of this amount is consumed alive.

Pacific oysters, the most common in the world

Most of the oysters produced in the world are Pacific oysters, which are also called gigas oysters, Japanese oysters or cupped oysters. Originally this oyster came from Asia, but the Pacific oyster has been moved to many places in the world. It has an oblong shell with an irregular surface, and the lower shell is deep, like a cup. It is well-suited to aquaculture. It is reasonably easy to make it reproduce in a controlled setting and on a large scale. It is robust, fast-growing and resistant against a number of diseases which have killed off other species of oysters in many places.

Pacific oysters were brought to Europe in the 1950s and 1960s. But the so-called Portuguese oyster, which has "always" been found along the Atlantic coast of France, Spain and Portugal, is a close relative of the Pacific oyster. From 1967 to 1971, the Portuguese oyster was nearly wiped out by disease. The Pacific oyster survived, and one theory is that the Pacific oyster was a carrier of the virus for this disease, but it did not catch it itself. Another theory is that the Portuguese oyster really is the Pacific oyster, brought to Europe by seafarers during Marco Polo's time, and that the same oyster has adapted and developed under different conditions in both parts of the world. Studies which have been done – both of preserved specimens which were kept from the time when the oyster disease broke out, and of the genes of the two types of oysters – indicate that both theories probably are

A bouquet of Norwegian bivalves and snails. Here you can see both round oysters and typically oval Pacific oysters, the large scallop as well as the smaller species of scallops, Iceland scallops, queen scallops and black scallops, small common mussels, large horse mussels and different types of clams.

correct. And history teaches us two things: that moving live animals can disrupt the sensitive balance between the animals and the endless and complex world of microbes around them; and that people have always brought food with them on journeys. Food which could be stored alive and fresh while they were on their journey, and food they related to. The use of oysters goes far, far back – to the roots of man.

European flat oysters: the best oyster in the world - having a hard time!

We can dig out oyster shells from the middens of Norwegian stone age settlements. The flat oyster was a primeval creature in our waters. It is a genuine part of European nature, a completely European species – widespread from the coast of Morocco north to Trøndelag. The flat oyster has more or less round, flat shells and a smoother surface than the Pacific oyster. The flat oyster is considered the best in the world for eating. At its very best – in winter – it can be sweet, robust and flavorful.

Unfortunately, the European flat oyster has come upon hard times. The climate in Scandinavia these days is a little too cold for this warmth-loving species to survive very well. The flat oyster needs water temperatures of around 18-20°C (64-68°F) for a good stretch in the spring and summer in order to reproduce. It cannot find that in open coastal Norwegian waters today, and therefore we find wild oysters only in polls, narrow bays and coves, and in shallow water which warms up during the summer.

There are some quite rich populations of oysters from Oslofjord down the coast of southern Norway, often at a couple of meters' depth – deep enough for them not to be destroyed by the movement of ice in the winter. Along the coast of western Norway, north to Trøndelag, there are a number of areas with small populations of oysters – more seldom the farther north we are – and active harvesting and sale of oysters along the coast of

The Aga poll at Bømlo in Hordaland is a traditional Norwegian oyster poll. Every summer, numerous collectors hang out in the poll to collect flat oyster spat in the traditional manner. To augment the classic production, a floating hatchery, a nursery and laboratory have been built on site. Old and new technology working together - the goal is to combine the best from the past and the future.

south and west Norway until the middle of the 19th century. When the climate became cooler, between 1850 and 1870, the great stocks of oysters disappeared. They were probably harvested faster than they could reproduce. Now the stocks in most places are so small that they cannot survive harvesting on any large scale. If you find any of these, take a few for your own use, but be careful and look upon the place as your own personal treasure chest.

In most areas south of Scandinavia, the flat oyster struggles with a completely different problem. The disease, bonamiosis, was introduced to France by live oysters from the US in 1979 and has been a plague on the flat oyster ever since. The rich stocks of flat oysters in Spain, France and the Netherlands have been reduced to a fraction of what they were prior to 1979. The problem has also arisen in England and Ireland. Scotland, Northern Ireland and Scandinavia remain untouched, and we can remain that way as long as no one illegally introduces live flat oysters to our waters. The Pacific oyster has an immune system which apparently handles the parasite, and it has now taken over production as well as most of the market in Europe.

Oyster farming, on a wave length with nature

Farming of flat oysters in Norway goes back to the 1880s, to the time after the wild stocks disappeared. In their work to find out how to reestablish oyster production, researchers discovered a number of polls along the coast with sizeable oyster stocks. During the years up to 1930, experiments were performed in these polls. Scientists discovered that when the sun warmed the water in the polls, they could turn into real oases for oysters. If a layer of brackish water forms on top of the sea water in a poll, it acts like a greenhouse

roof. The sun heats the water in the poll during the day. The layer of brackish water retains the water heated by the sun – the warmth is not released during the night, and the water down in the poll becomes much warmer than that on the surface. It can keep an even temperature around the clock and through a long summer season. People learned to take advantage of these special conditions and established methods for harvesting large quantities of spat from the polls. This led to the development of an industry which has continued to the present day. Even though shellfish farmers today develop hatcheries and modern methods of farming, the principles for producing oyster spat are the same as the were 100 years ago – mainly something so elementary as working in tune with nature and with the flat oyster's own distinctive biology.

Love in every bite!

Oysters are the world's best known aphrodisiac. Known from Greek and Roman pre-Christian history for its divine effect, alive in French cuisine today, loved and recognized – but why? Let's forget about the nourishing qualities for a while. That's altogether too scientific for this discussion. The appearance, perhaps? The sight of a live oyster – or even a mussel – which lies under water and draws in water through a small opening in its mantle, surrounded by undulating lips and mantle, is a beautiful sight – which easily leads thoughts to a woman's genitals. And both color and looks are important with most aphrodisiacs. Or perhaps the reason is that oysters and cool, refreshing, fruity white wine are light, pleasant food, which does not make us feel heavy, slow, lazy and indifferent. We should use our energy to have fun, not to digest food. Is it because oysters contain the substance dopamine – which is important for the transferral of nerve impulses, which

Crate upon crate of Norwegian Pacific oysters stand in fresh running water at the Sealife packing plant, at Tysnes in Hordaland, ready to be sent to market.

work on brain activity and influence desire? Or is it the high zinc content – a substance needed for the production of sperm – which does that? What do we know!? The most important thing is that it works – at any rate, we are convinced that it does. And in addition, what is more healthy and fun than a reason to compose a tempting meal with a good nachspiel?

"They taste like sea water"

Those who don't like oysters say that they taste like sea water. Those who love oysters say the same thing. Oysters taste like the sea. They are supposed to, they have to taste of the sea. That is a sign of freshness. But they should not taste of only sea water. If so, the oyster is too light and not good to eat. It should taste of much, much more, and it should have

You really only need two tools: an oyster knife with a sturdy short blade to open oysters, and a small sharp knife to loosen the adductor muscle of the scallop from its shell, and to cut up the meat.

Open oysters either by guiding the oyster knife between the shells at the side, or at the point of the shells, as illustrated here. Hold the oyster stable, preferably in a towel. Do not press hard, but move the knife sideways until the hinge breaks, then remove the flat shell.

Then you cut the adductor muscle loose from the other shell, and it is ready to serve or cook.

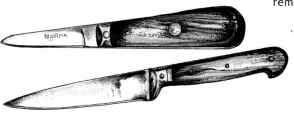

a fresh, almost vegetal flavor from all the algae it has consumed in the sea, be pleasantly salty, sweet from the sweetening agent glycogen, which it stores through summer and fall, and have a more or less pronounced metallic aftertaste. Most people have to get accustomed to the flavor of oysters, After that, oysters are among the best food which can be presented on a platter of seafood.

Oysters are winter food

In France, two-thirds of the yearly oyster production is consumed in December. In Norway, oysters are not such a part of the cuisine that they have a particular season, as do crabs. But both flavor and meatiness of the oyster changes over the course of the year, and the variations can be quite great. The quality changes with the maturation process and its access to food in the sea. During the summer and fall, there is rich algae growth in the sea, and the shells have all the food they need. Then they build up a store of nourishment which they can use over the winter. Much of this nourishment is stored as glycogen, a kind of sugar. When a good autumn is almost over, the temperature in the sea sinks, the thick growth of algae is gone and winter is on its way, the oyster is

sweet, flavorful and meaty. When it is cold, the oyster uses its stored energy reserves, but at the same time slows down and can retain its top quality over the winter. With spring comes a change: The sun gradually warms the sea water, algae begin to bloom in the nourishing water. Nature wakes up again and the shells change their metabolism. Now it is time to reproduce. The energy reserves in the shells are used to produce roe and sperm, and fat is transferred to these reproductive cells. Said simply, the flavor of the oyster changes from sweet to oily. The oysters are not so attractive any more – at least they are not eaten raw. After spawning, the oyster is usually rather empty and watery. Then the myth that oysters "taste like seawater" can be quite true.

Every rule has its exception. Oysters require quite high water temperatures to mature and spawn. In Norway, they are often cultivated in cold water in open sea and therefore do not undergo a natural maturation

process. The changes in quality are not so pronounced, and the oyster can be acceptable also in low season. The problem is that cultivation and quality control of bivalves in Norway have not been properly standardized. We do not find out what kind of product we have purchased before the shells have entered the kitchen, and then it is too late. During the summer, it is just as well to accept that it is low season for a while.

Oysters - in different qualities

In France, both flat oysters and Pacific oysters are marketed in a spectrum of classes. In the Marennes-Oléron area on the French Atlantic coast, quality grading has been standardized. Here, the landscape along the shore is more water than land – one great large mosaic of pools. The pools are shallow basins supplied with seawater through a system of canals. They can be filled up at spring tide and closed off. Originally they were used for the extraction of valuable sea salt. Today they are used in oyster production. The conditions in such pools can be ideal for producing perfect oysters. We should be familiar with the principle, since oyster production in our own natural polls was initiated more than

100 years ago, partly based on experience from using basins in central Europe.

Green oysters are great

The cultivated oyster is cleaned, sorted and put into crates which are placed on the bottom of the pools for "affinage". Affinage is difficult to translate. We would like to say for "fattening up" but that is wrong, because a "fatty" taste has negative connotations. This is all about refinement, a last phase which gives the oyster "that little extra something."

Algae, which bloom in the pools, encourage the oyster to gain weight, and its flavor changes. Glycogen is an important component of the oyster's stored nourishment, and when the amount of glycogen increases, the flavor becomes sweeter. In addition, the types of algae also influence the flavor of the oyster. The salty, fresh and slightly sharp flavor of the sea in the gray oyster out on the banks is tempered and complemented with more sweetness, improved mass and a slight vegetal flavor like fresh seaweed – in other words, more flavor, a more complex flavor picture and less salt – and not least, a completely different color. The oyster's gills turn green "Then it's a good season!" This does not always happen, but when it does, it makes oyster fans happy. This unusual change in color takes place due to a microscopic a diatom algae called *Navicula ostrearia*. It is excellent food for the oyster, and in addition to all the important nutrients, it also contains a pigment which the shells absorb. After filtering water for this algae, for a while, the gills of the oyster gradually turn color.

The French are not necessarily so enthusiastic about green seafood. But they are enthusiastic about flavor and for the special characteristics of the product. If *Navicula ostrearia* blooms

in the pools – and the oysters turn green – you have concrete evidenced that the oyster has experienced "affinage". This is important, for the Pacific oyster is sold in a number of categories. It is classified and marketed in a semi-official system based on three criteria. The first and simplest is size, or more correctly stated, weight. Oysters are classified in defined weights and numbered accordingly.

The second criterion is grade of "affinage". They oysters can be wild and, in practice, harvested anywhere, come from oyster banks or from "affinage" in the pools. The latter can either be "fines de claire" or "speciales de claire". There are rules for how long and in which density shells can remain in a pool to be classified as "fines" and "speciales".

The third criterion is less official and concerns origin. The French consider where the oyster was produced as the deciding factor in its flavor and quality. The connection with its origin are a kind of unofficial "appellation de origin contrôlée, perhaps best known and widespread in the classification of wine. Marennes-Oléron has become a well-known expression for Pacific oysters. Another example of the impor-

A "speciale de claire" from the Marennes-Oléron area. Pacific oysters cannot be more beautiful, greener or better than this.

tant "little extra" attached to origin are flat oysters from the Belon area of Brittany. The flat oysters from here are considered extra fine, and "belons" are in many places so well-established, that the term means flat oysters.

When oysters are sold in a French market, an open oyster is placed on top of the crate. A crate of closed oysters tells the customer nothing about what she or he is purchasing. The open oysters are the seller's display and the buyer's guarantee. We should learn to do this here, too. Crates with live, meaty oysters with green gills almost sell themselves. The color is a seal of quality and a guarantee that the oyster is a genuine "Marennes-Oléron". It is also important to give each product an identity. While we - altogether too often strive to make our products uniform, in France, people appreciate a broad selection. Producers in different regions emphasize their regional identity, how the character of the area – "terroir" –

influences the product, whether it is a wine or an oyster.

Oysters in the kitchen. What now?

For many, the biggest challenge with an oyster is opening it. It is easy with the right equipment. And that means no screwdrivers, kitchen knives or pocket knives. We have seen cuts on fingers, broken knife tips and ruined oysters – all caused by the lack of a proper oyster knife. The oyster knife is an invaluable tool for a shellfish lover. A short blade in good-quality steel that does not break, with a compact, round shaft which sits well in the hand. And now the technique: As indicated on the illustration, place the oyster in a cloth, paper or towel in your left hand – if you are right-handed. Aim the point of the knife into the pointed end where the two shells meet. Don't press too hard – then the knife will go right into your thumb, if you lose your grip – just move the knife up and down sideways until the hinge breaks. Then you can guide the knife along the inside of the flat shell and cut over the adductor muscle. An alternative is to break a little of the

shell on one side, as near to the muscle as possible and find an opening between the shells there. When the muscle is cut over, the oyster is open. Cut over the muscle in the deep shell as well, to make the oyster consumer-friendly. You can eat everything inside the shell.

And then the choice of wine!

A toast to the oyster opener, and then to the guests. Choosing a wine for oysters is not so complicated. A number of types of wine work well with oysters. But it's a good idea to choose wines which are dry, but at the same time which harmonize well with the fresh, salty flavor of the sea and metallic aftertaste of the oyster. If we look at how oysters are served in France, we find a number of excellent combinations. Oysters and Champagne are a classic and literally, a beguiling combination. Perfect for an evening of temptation – as long as the chosen one likes oysters – and for serving fresh oysters raw as a first course in an elegant meal. Another classic French combination is oysters and Chablis. Chablis has a rather flinty, mineral flavor which backs-up oysters well, and in a way reinforces their metallic character. Chablis has been a stylish wine for a while now, and it has experienced some inflation. Not everything in a Chablis bottle is equally exciting, so it is a good idea to be a little critical and selective in picking out a bottle. Wines from the upper part of the Loire valley can also be an excellent choice: Sancerre can also have a mineral flavor component which suits oysters perfectly. At the same time, the fresh and slightly sour fruit, gooseberry and citrus elements provide a fresh and comfortable contrast to the saltiness of the shellfish. When we have been

able to get a good Sancerre "Vieilles Vignes" (from old vines) and have served it with warm, flavorful, sweet flat oysters in a creamy sauce, the result has been wonderfully harmonious – and very well received.

In the Bordeaux region, which is just within Europe's major production area for oysters, local, dry white wines from Entre Deux Mers and Graves are paired with oysters. A good white Graves is a wonderful wine, with freshness, suppleness, acidity and enough body to complement just about any shellfish dish.

At a New Year's party in Brittany, together with some Breton friends, we have experienced oysters and wine in all their simple elegance. With bread, butter, a few crates of Pacific oysters from the best producer, at their seasonal best, accompanied by a couple of cases of excellent young, fresh Muscadet sur lie, produced by the father of one of my French friends – and most certainly from their own, best vintage. Simple and stylish. With the bone dry wine, which in itself had a slightly salty flavor, neither the oysters nor the wine were too filling, and they really complemented one another. The wine made the oysters light and fresh to eat – and the shells invited us to have an extra glass. Outside, in the cool night, the wind blew from the Bay of Biscay, and France smelled of the salty sea.

RAW OYSTERS

When serving raw oysters, count on 6-12 oysters per person, depending upon whether you plan to serve other appetizers or courses, whether they are "snacks" or part of a larger meal.

You can eat oysters just as they are. Raw oysters are fresh and good. It is a meaningless misunderstanding, if you think that you have to swallow oysters whole and fast. Of course, you are supposed to chew them. How else will you be able to experience their heavenly flavor? Don't throw away their juices, either. If they're not too salty, you can drink them, too. Raw oysters are often served with a few drops of lemon juice and a little freshly ground pepper. It doesn't have to be more difficult than that. An exciting alternative is to make a dip or two. There are a few classics, such as mignonette sauce, made of shallot, lemon juice, red wine vinegar and freshly ground black pepper, and chile sauce, made with the same ingredients plus green chile, coriander and a little sugar. Here are a few suggestions for dips which can add an exciting flavor to oysters. Each dip is enough for 15 oysters.

Red wine vinegar-shallot dip

3 tablespoons minced shallot
3 tablespoons red wine vinegar
salt and pepper

Combine shallot and vinegar and season with salt and pepper.

Coriander-lime dip

2 tablespoons minced shallot
1/2 garlic clove, minced
1/2 teaspoon minced red chile pepper
1/2 teaspoon minced ginger
2 tablespoons fresh lime juice
1 teaspoon chopped fresh coriander
5 tablespoons (1/3 cup) olive oil
salt and pepper

Combine all ingredients.

Hot pepper-herb dip

1/2 tablespoon minced fresh coriander
1/2 tablespoon minced fresh chervil
1 tablespoon minced shallot
up to 1/2 tablespoon Louisiana hot pepper sauce
1 tablespoon fresh lemon juice
2 tablespoons olive oil

Combine herbs and shallot. Whisk in remaining ingredients.

Lemon-celery salsa

2 tablespoons peeled and chopped celery
2 tablespoons minced shallot
2 tablespoons olive oil
2 tablespoons chopped lemon (no pits, no rind)
salt and freshly ground pepper

Newly opened, fresh oysters. Choose between flat, round flat oysters or more oblong, deeper Pacific oysters.

Combine all ingredients.

BEVERAGE SUGGESTION

Serve with a cold, dry white wine, Muscadet, wine from Gascogne or other areas of southern France. A white Bordeaux, such as Entre Deux Mers, is also good with raw oysters.

49

HEAT-TREATED OYSTERS

You can also steam, grill, bake and fry oysters, and you can use them as a flavoring agent in other seafood dishes. Oysters are loved all over the world, so it is only natural that there are an infinite number of ways to prepare them. Some dishes are classics and can be found in many cookbooks. Try Oysters Rockefeller, with its wonderful combination of oysters and spinach, or "angels on horseback" in which oysters are rolled in a bacon slice and grilled. Here are a few recipes which showcase oysters in several ways.

STEAMED OYSTERS WITH ASPARAGUS AND LEMON

12 oysters
2 tablespoons oyster juices
1 dl (1/2 cup) whipping cream
1 shallot, minced
1/2 teaspoon Dijon mustard
1 tablespoon unsalted butter
chopped flat-leaf parsley
chopped chives

12 asparagus
2 tablespoons olive oil
salt and pepper
1 teaspoon lemon juice

Open oysters, remove meat and reserve juices. Place meat in a saucepan with 2 tablespoons of the juices. Pour remaining juices in another saucepan, add cream and shallot and reduce over high heat until half the original amount remains. Whisk in mustard and butter.

Steam oysters carefully and add to cream sauce. Season with herbs.

Peel asparagus and sauté in oil over medium heat. Season with salt and pepper. Just before serving, stir in lemon juice. Arrange on plates. Ladle over oyster cream sauce.

DEEP-FRIED OYSTERS WITH BASIL MAYONNAISE

approximately 8 oysters per person
fresh breadcrumbs
chopped parsley
minced garlic

all-purpose flour
beaten egg

Open oysters, remove meat and dry with paper towels. Then the breading will stick to them easier. Season breadcrumbs with parsley and garlic. Dip dry oysters first in flour, then in beaten egg and last in breadcrumbs. Refrigerate until time to fry.

Basil mayonnaise

1 egg yolk
2 tablespoons white wine vinegar
1 tablespoon lemon juice
1 tablespoon Dijon mustard
1 tablespoon minced shallot
5-6 tablespoons (1/3 cup) chopped fresh basil
3 dl (1 1/4 cups) corn oil
salt and pepper

Place all ingredients, excluding oil in a food processor and puree for a few seconds. With motor running, add oil in a thin stream until emulsified. Season with salt and pepper.

Deep-fried vegetables

broccoli
cauliflower
celery
1 egg
1 1/4 dl (1/2 cup) white wine
2 1/2 dl (1 cup) all-purpose flour
corn or soybean oil

Clean vegetables, drying well. Cut broccoli and cauliflower into small florets, celery into 5-6 cm (2") lengths. Whisk together egg and white wine. Whisk in flour. Let batter rest about 10 minutes. Heat oil to 170°C (350°F). Dip vegetables in batter and deep-fry until golden, about 3 minutes. Drain on paper towels.

Deep-fry oysters about one minute. Drain on paper towels. Serve oysters and vegetables with mayonnaise in small bowls alongside.

OYSTERS AU GRATIN

There are many versions of this dish. The easiest is probably to dot each oyster with lemon butter (unsalted butter beaten with freshly ground pepper, lemon peel, lemon juice and dill) and place under the broiler. Here we bread the oysters and serve them with wasabi butter. Wasabi is a strong Japanese horseradish.

OYSTERS WITH WASABI BUTTER

16 oysters
coarse sea salt
1 teaspoon wasabi
120 g (4 oz) unsalted butter
fresh breadcrumbs

Preheat oven to 250°C (450°F). Open oysters and loosen from shell as illustrated on page 46. Leave oysters in bottom shells. Place on a bed of sea salt on an oven tray. Combine wasabi and butter and place a small amount on each oyster. Bake two minutes. Remove from oven and sprinkle with breadcrumbs. Bake until light golden, about one minute. Serve immediately.

OYSTERS WITH JULIENNE VEGETABLES AND BEURRE BLANC

In this recipe, we serve oysters with finely shredded vegetables "julienne" and a classic French "beurre blanc" butter sauce. Count on 5 oysters per person as an appetizer. You can use this dish as a main course by adding steamed flat fish, haddock, wolffish or small pieces of sautéed monkfish.

20 oysters

Beurre blanc

2 tablespoons minced shallot
2 tablespoons butter
1 dl (1/2 cup) white wine
3 tablespoons whipping cream

juice from oysters
125 g (4 oz) unsalted butter

Julienne

1 small carrot
1/2 leek
2 celery stalks
2 shallots

Open oysters and reserve bottom shells. Pour juices into a measuring cup.

Prepare sauce as described in basic recipes, page 107.

Clean and shred vegetables. Blanch in lightly salted water about 15 seconds. Remove and drain on paper towels. Simmer oysters about 10 seconds in the same water. Return oysters to shells and top with vegetables. Spoon hot sauce over oysters and vegetables and serve immediately.

BEVERAGE SUGGESTION

A white wine with a little body – preferably a Chardonnay, is good with this dish. If you are having a party, there's nothing wrong with serving it with a bottle of Champagne!

ICELAND SCALLOPS

a taste sensation from icy waters

Iceland scallops are a nordic scallop species which reaches a maximum size of about 11 cm (4 1/2"). It can be distinguished easily from the king scallop because it has two curved, ribbed shells and asymmetrical "ears" at the shell points. Usually it is a reddish-gold color.

The distribution of Iceland scallops is primarily determined by water temperature. Today, the largest stocks are found in Norway north of the Lofoten islands and in the northern regions around Jan Mayen, Spitsbergen and Bear Island. In northern Norway, there are banks of Iceland scallops in some fjords, usually on a hard bottom between 15 and 60 meters (50 and 200 feet) deep. Farther south, there are isolated stocks in some fjords, and perhaps most remarkably, in the enclosed Lindås polls north of Bergen. These are so-called "relic" stocks – survivors from the period around the last ice age, when water temperature along the coast was lower, and the Iceland scallop had a much wider distribution. In many places we can find shells which indicate that Iceland scallops were found in areas far away from where they are today.

Iceland scallops in the fjords are harvested with shell scrapers during the autumn and winter seasons. Small numbers are also harvested by divers. The Iceland scallop has been the most important variety of scallop in Norway for many years, with a total volume between one and two thousand tons per year.

A sad chapter about resource management

The large Iceland scallop stocks around Bear Island and Spitsbergen were discovered when ships from the Norwegian Institute of Marine Research were doing test fishing in the northern regions during the 1960s and 1970s. Harvesting did not begin until 1985, when seafaring vessels found great quantities of Iceland scallops near Jan Mayen. Between 1986 and 1989, the University of Tromsø and the Institute of Marine Research in Bergen made investigations which mapped out a number of areas with rich stocks of scallops. In 1985, there were only a few vessels harvesting there, but good catches which paid well attracted

The beautiful red color of the Iceland scallop is a sharp contrast against the dark ocean floor.

55

others. In 1986 and 1987, the number of ships had risen to 27. Some were large, converted factory trawlers with more than 30 men onboard, equipped to harvest with several scrapers simultaneously. Onboard was a complete processing factory with freezers, and the trawlers had the capacity to fish over a ton of shellfish every four hours while in operation. The ships brought in the catch as frozen blocks of just the white muscle. In 1987, 45,000 tons of Iceland scallops were harvested, with a value of more than 150 million kroner (USD 19 million). Neither the stocks of scallops nor the market itself could handle this. The fields were so stripped that it no longer paid for large expensive factory ships to work there anymore, and the market was oversaturated.

Regulations restricting harvesting, which were implemented from 1986, came too late. After free harvesting for a couple of seasons, the "adventure" was over. By 1989, most of the fields were closed, and during the last few years, one single ship has harvested Iceland scallops in northern waters. This is an example of exploitation of resources which could not support itself. A couple of ships probably could have harvested sensibly, possibly forever. A whole fleet could not do this. It is better with scallops on the sea bed than in a freezer warehouse.

Queen scallops and black scallops

There are also other species of small scallops along the coast, but they are not harvested commercially. The queen scallop is quite common. It is similar to the Iceland scallop, but it has fewer and more finely curved ribs in its shell. It is found along the coast as far north as Troms, from a few meters depth to around 200 meters (660 feet). Queen scallops are harvested by shell scrapers around the British Isles.

We can also find black scallops in shallower water. They sometimes live just below the tidal zone and can be found along the coast as far north as Troms. Black scallops are often fixed in place,

and they can vary in color. They are usually gray or gray-brown, but we can also find yellow and violet specimens. Black scallops have tight ribs, and the front ear is much larger than the back one.

Farming of Iceland and queen scallops

Farming of both Iceland and queen scallops has been attempted on a trial basis. It is based on the collection of spat from wild stocks. The spat are set out in baskets which hang in the sea from lines stretched under the surface of the water. Aquaculture of Iceland scallops, which was attempted in northern Norway in the 1980s, was reasonably successful, but it was discontinued because of uncertain supplies of spat and low profitability. Today, new attempts are being made at collecting spat and measuring growth to see if there may be a basis for Iceland scallop farming in some areas of northern Norway.

Where do we find raw materials?

There is a large international market for the small scallop varieties. Iceland scallops from Norway, Canada and Iceland, queen scallops from Great Britain, similar varieties from the Antarctic Sea, China, New Zealand, Chile and other places

compete in this market. These shellfish are usually sold as frozen muscle or frozen muscle with roe. They often end up in different consumer-friendly variations of frozen seafood and ready-meals.

In countries where there is great demand for fresh shellfish, the small varieties of scallops are sold fresh, alongside king scallops. In Norway, there has not been a large enough market for the small species. Iceland scallops are marketed sporadically. We can just hope that these shellfish will be more available in the future. If we ask wholesalers to get them for us, can we be sure that they will do that?

Dishes with Iceland scallops, queen scallops and black scallops

Small scallops taste just as good as large. They have that same sweet flavor. Fresh, they cannot be beaten and are even sweeter and more flavorful than their larger relative. If they are of good quality and have not been frozen for too long, they can be an exciting and versatile ingredient in all kinds of dishes.

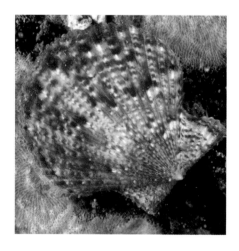

The queen scallop, a common species of scallop, which reaches a maximum of 9 cm (4") , is found along most of the Norwegian coast.

The black scallop has barbs along its shell ridges, and one ear is much larger than the other.

OPEN RAVIOLI WITH GRILLED ICELAND SCALLOPS AND TINY TOMATOES

Tomato sauce

25 small tomatoes or cherry tomatoes
1 shallot
2 garlic cloves
2 tablespoons butter
1 dl (1/2 cup) white wine
1 dl (1/2 cup) whipping cream
3 dl (1 1/2 cups) fish stock
(see basic recipes page 111)

Preheat oven to 200°C (400°F). Bake tomatoes 15-20 minutes. Mince shallot and garlic and sauté in butter until shiny. Add wine and reduce until 1/3 of the original amount remains. Add 5 baked tomatoes, cream and stock. Bring to a boil, then mix with an immersion blender until frothy or puree in a food processor.

4 pasta sheets (15x15 cm/6x6")
(see pasta recipe page 108)

Cook pasta in lightly salted water.

500 g (1 lb) fresh spinach
1 garlic clove
4 tablespoons (1/4 cup) olive oil

Wash spinach thoroughly. Remove coarse stalks. Mince garlic. Sauté in oil in a hot pan. Season with salt and pepper.

20 large Iceland scallops
olive oil or walnut oil
salt and pepper

Sauté scallops in oil about one minute per side.

Arrange spinach in center of deep plates with tomatoes and scallops all around. Cover with pasta and spoon over sauce.

ICELAND SCALLOPS WITH POTATO CHIPS AND GREEN BEANS

Iceland scallops

24 Iceland scallops
oil
ground coriander
salt and pepper

Open scallops, loosen muscle from shell and from surrounding parts. Dry with paper towels. Sauté just before serving. Iceland scallops do not require long preparation time. They should be served with a raw center.

Potato chips

2 baking potatoes
1 liter (4 cups) vegetable oil
salt

Peel potatoes and slice as thinly as possible. Rinse to remove starch. Dry well. Heat oil to 170°C (350°F) and deep-fry until golden 1-2 minutes. Drain on paper towels. Sprinkle with salt.

Beans

70 g (2 1/2 oz) green beans
salt

Clean and rinse beans. Cook in salted (1/2 teaspoon per dl (1/2 cup)) water. Salt content should be almost like seawater, because green vegetables need more salt during cooking than other vegetables to retain flavor and their fine green color.

Tomato-olive vinaigrette

4 black olives
2 dried tomatoes
1 shallot
3 tablespoons extra virgin olive oil
1 tablespoon balsamic vinegar
salt and freshly ground pepper
lemon juice, if necessary

Clean olives, tomatoes and shallot. Cut into fine dice and place in a bowl. Whisk together oil and vinegar and pour over vegetables. Season with salt and pepper and a little lemon juice. Do not use too much salt – dried tomatoes and olives are both salty.

Layer scallops, potato chips and green beans. Serve with tomato-olive vinaigrette.

ICELAND SCALLOP TOURNEDOS WITH BULGUR, LIME AND MINT

In this dish, we fit 5 or 6 scallops in a form lined with daikon radish (or you can use parsnip, blanched leek or asparagus) to make a tournedo. These are served with bulgur, which is made of cracked wheat, but you can also serve them with rice, pasta or couscous.

Iceland scallop tournedos

20-24 Iceland scallops

1 daikon (long white) radish
ground star anise
oil
salt and freshly ground white pepper

Open scallops, loosen mussel from shell and surrounding parts. Peel radish and slice 4 thin strips length-wise. Blanch in lightly salt water for about 30 seconds. Cool and dry. Use a metal ring/form about 7 cm (3") in diameter to hold scallops and radish in place. Place a band of radish along edge of ring. Cut off excess radish. Arrange scallops in ring and sprinkle with star anise, salt and freshly ground pepper. Just before serving, dry with paper towels and sauté on both sides in oil with ring/form in place.

Bulgur

1 1/2 dl (2/3 cup) bulgur
1 1/2 dl (2/3 cup) water
2 tablespoons olive oil
1/2 teaspoon chopped mint
juice and grated zest of 1 lime
salt and freshly ground white pepper

Place bulgur in a bowl. Bring water and olive oil to a boil and pour over bulgur. Stir in mint, lime juice and zest, salt and pepper. Cover with plastic wrap and let mixture marinate for 10-15 minutes, so bulgur can absorb liquid. Press into a ring before serving.

Tomato vinaigrette

1 shallot
1 tablespoon tomato paste
1 dl (scant 1/2 cup) olive oil
2 tablespoons lemon juice
salt and freshly ground white pepper

Peel and mince shallot. Combine with tomato paste and lemon juice. Whisk in olive oil in drops until emulsified. Season with lemon juice, salt and pepper.

Place bulgur in center of four plates. Top with scallops. Drizzle tomato vinaigrette all around.

ICELAND SCALLOPS WITH SHIITAKE, SPRING ONIONS AND LEMON BUTTER

Here is a combination of shellfish and mushrooms. Any other firm mushroom can be used in place of shiitake mushrooms.

24 Iceland scallops
oil, butter
salt and freshly ground pepper

16 shiitake mushrooms
1 dl (1/3 cup) water
1 tablespoon butter
salt

6 spring onions
1 dl (1/3 cup) water
1 tablespoon butter
salt

1 tablespoon sugar
juice of 1 lemon
3 tablespoons cold butter
salt and freshly ground pepper

Iceland scallops

Open scallops, loosen muscle from shell and surrounding parts. Dry with paper towels. Sauté in oil and butter just before serving. Season with salt and pepper.

Vegetables

Steam mushrooms and spring onions separately in water with butter and salt for 5-7 and 2 minutes respectively. If cooked in the same saucepan, they lose some flavor and color.

Lemon butter sauce

Caramelize sugar in the smallest saucepan. Add lemon juice. Reduce until 1/4 of the original amount remains. Reduce heat. Beat in butter and season with salt and pepper. Add more lemon juice, if necessary.

Drain vegetables and arrange on plates with scallops. Serve with a spoonful of lemon butter sauce. Garnish with dill fronds, if desired.

ICELAND SCALLOP CEVICHE WITH ENDIVE AND HORSERADISH CREAM

Ceviche is a South American dish in which fish or seafood are marinated and "cooked" in citrus juice. The acid in citrus fruits changes the proteins in fish and shellfish, so they get a firmer, almost cooked texture. This dish is easy to make. The scallops are marinated and served in endive leaves with a fine contrast of horseradish cream alongside. The endive is mostly used as a decorative and practical means of presentation, but it also adds flavor. You can also make this dish with other kinds of scallops.

Marinade

2 tablespoons fresh lemon juice
2 tablespoons fresh lime juice
1 tablespoon chopped coriander
2 tablespoons tomato concassé
(see page 109)
1 baked garlic clove
(see page 106), crushed
4 tablespoons (1/4 cup)
extra virgin olive oil

Combine all ingredients.

12 Iceland scallops
8 endive leaves

Cut scallops in two or more slices and add to marinade. The longer they marinate, the more they change flavor and texture. Around 30 minutes is about right.

Clean and wash endive. Soak in ice water for 10 minutes to make flavor milder.

Horseradish cream

1/2 dl (3 1/2 tablespoons) crème fraiche or dairy sour cream
2 tablespoons milk
1 teaspoon sugar
2 tablespoons grated horseradish
1 teaspoon fresh lime juice
1 tablespoon chopped chives
salt and pepper

Whisk all ingredients together.

Arrange marinated scallops in endive slices. Garnish with fresh herbs and serve with horseradish cream.

BEVERAGE SUGGESTION

Green tea is a good choice.

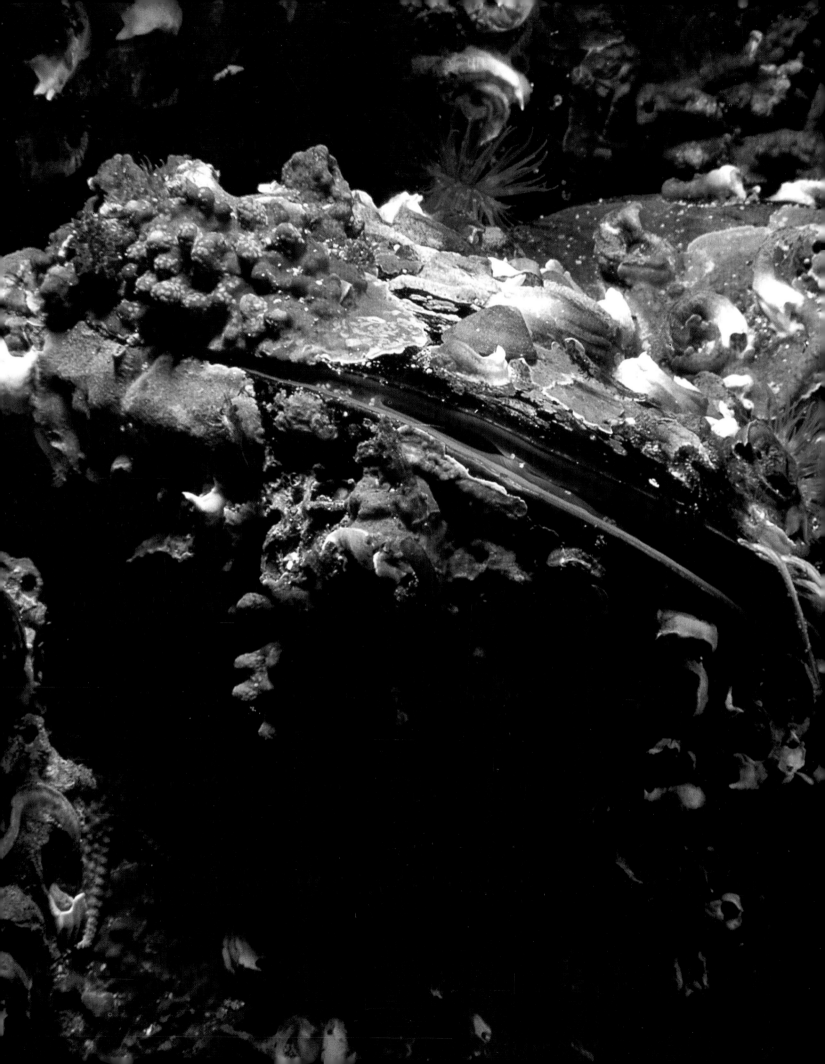

HORSE MUSSELS
a temptation in living color

At first glance, horse mussels look much like common mussels, but with a closer examination, we see that they are different from their smaller relative in many ways. Horse mussels are usually rounder, and shell features more red or brown nuances. The hinge which holds the two shells together sits a little to the side of the point, not at the point, as it does on a common mussel. Horse mussels grow larger than most other edible bivalves in our waters, and the average size of those harvested is 10-14 cm (4-7"). One reason why they have to be relatively large when harvested is that they do not mature until they are at least three years old, and often not before they are five to seven, and the edible parts are not large enough until then. Many years can pass between each time horse mussels spawn, so supplies can be stable over long periods of time, rather unaffected by seasonal variations as is the case with common mussels, oysters and scallops.

Where do we find horse mussels?

Horse mussels are a northern species, found on both sides of the Atlantic Ocean and also in the Pacific. In Europe, they are found from the coast of central France north to the White Sea, around the British Isles, the Faeroes and Iceland. They are found along the entire Norwegian coastline. While common mussels thrive in brackish water, horse mussels prefer salty ocean water, so we seldom find the two species in the same place. We can find horse mussels all the way from tidal waters to a depth of many hundred meters, often partially buried in sand and gravel, in kelp forests and on rocky bottoms, where there is a powerful current. In places with optimal growing conditions, horse mussels form great banks. They sit on the bottom, fastened to it and to one another with their strong byssal threads. They are not always easy to pull apart. The large compact mollusks can be more than

After sitting in the same place for 19 years, the horse mussel almost blends into the background, overgrown with algae and other creatures of the ocean floor. The characteristic orange-red mantle edge gives it away.

65

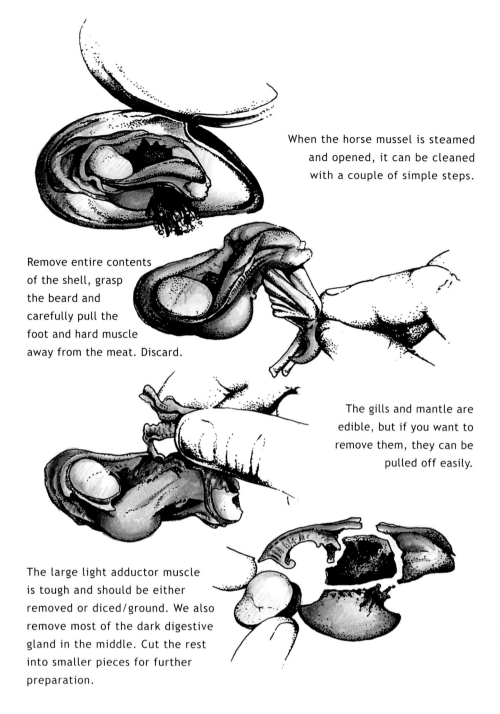

When the horse mussel is steamed and opened, it can be cleaned with a couple of simple steps.

Remove entire contents of the shell, grasp the beard and carefully pull the foot and hard muscle away from the meat. Discard.

The gills and mantle are edible, but if you want to remove them, they can be pulled off easily.

The large light adductor muscle is tough and should be either removed or diced/ground. We also remove most of the dark digestive gland in the middle. Cut the rest into smaller pieces for further preparation.

twenty years old. In western Norway, we have found and harvested good quality horse mussels in water so shallow that it is almost dry at low tide. Usually the banks are a little harder to reach, so harvesting has to be done from a boat with a rake or other equipment, or by diving.

An exciting piece of Norwegian history

Horse mussels have been an important species for Norwegian fisheries. During some years before World War II, the turnover for horse mussels was about NOK 500,000 – that was a lot of money in those days. They were not used for food, however, but as bait. Petter Dass, a famous Norwegian priest and poet from Nordland, wrote in one of his poems, that the haddock was "tempted by the reddish shell". He was referring to the horse mussel, which for a very long time – perhaps all the way back to the 16th century – was used as longline bait. Production of shellfish for bait was an important activity, and horse mussels were the most important resource. In shallow water, they were either harvested with tongs on a long shaft, with a two-armed shellfish-tong or a scraper, which was a long shaft connected to a steel hoe and a net bag which collected the shells. A shellfish plow was used in deeper water. This was a kind of rake with steel teeth which harvested the shells from the ocean floor. There were different variations of these scrapers, which were modified for specific locations and currents. They required several men and two boats at a time. One boat was anchored and drew the plow with a winch, while another was over and behind the plow and lifted it with a rope when it got stuck on the ocean floor. Attempts were also made to use divers for harvesting horse mussels, but it was too demanding and unprofitable. Harvesting of shellfish for bait usually took place from autumn to spring. The shells were opened with a knife, and beard, gills and mantle were cut away. The rest of the contents were placed in a loosely-woven basket so water could drain off. Then they were salted in barrels or kegs which could be stored and transported to wherever there was a market for bait. Bait harvesting took place along the entire coast, but it was most extensive on the west coast around Bergen, in Trøndelag and in Nordland. Horse mussels from Bergen were the most important bait used during the Lofoten cod fishing for many years. The statistics and yearly reports from Norwegian fisheries from 1869 to the second world war contain quite a bit of information: about the harvesting of horse mussels and other types of shellfish used for bait, about the fields of horse mussels, about exploitation and over-exploitation, discussions regarding management of supplies, prices, markets and trends. Marine researcher Kristian Fredrik Wiborg collected much of this data in a study of horse mussels published in 1946. After the war, harvesting shells for bait became outdated, especially during the early 1950s, when freezing technology made it more practical to use other types of bait, such as herring, squid and shrimp. Today, harvesting mussels for bait is a thing of the past – but now, if you find a scraper, tongs or plow in an old boathouse, you know what it was used for.

Cleaning and preparation

It is practical to steam horse mussels until they open, and then remove the meat. When the shell is opened, the difference from the common mussel is even greater. When we begin to work with the horse mussel in the kitchen, it has its own features and qualities. The digestive system is dark, and the muscles are a creamy white. The meat of male mussels is reddish yellow, females red orange. In shells which have spawned, most of the color is gone, and the meat is deflated and uninteresting.

It is most common to remove the mantle edge and the brownish gills, even though they are edible. The muscles are then removed. They are tough and should be ground or diced before eating. They are often discarded. If you hold the shelled mussel in one hand and pull the beard with the other, the muscle along the length of the mussel and the foot can be pulled out with a simple gesture. The rest of the mussel can be used, but it is a good idea to remove at least most of the digestive system. A large horse mussel may have filtered the sea water around it for more than twenty years and absorbed everything nature had to offer, good and bad. If the mussel has accumulated heavy metals or poisons, they are stored in the digestive system. Horse mussels are known to harbor more heavy metals than other bivalves. If we are going to eat a lot of shellfish, it is a good idea to limit our intake of those parts which we know can contain the least healthy substances. What we are left with after removing mantle, gills, muscles and most of the digestive system is colorful, delicate and has a distinctive, fresh flavor.

Pearls - No thanks!

My first attempt at a creative shellfish dish was with a group of boys when I was a teenager. We went diving for flounder and horse mussels on a lazy, hot summer day. We steamed them open and used them as pizza topping. We enjoyed a few beers while the dinner was cooking. Young boys, empty stomachs, tired and exhausted bodies after a day of fresh air, swimming and diving – we were a bit out of it when the pizza was ready. It smelled wonderful. As we bit into our slices simultaneously, we heard the strangest crunching noises from between our teeth. The mussels were full of pearls. They sat so closely together along the mantle that they made the mussels inedible. Some pearls were as tiny as grains of sand, while others were almost as big as peppercorns. The rest of the meal consisted of cheese and crackers.

Now we know. The horse mussels of our youth were gathered from a small bank in a bay where the tide constantly moved sand and gravel back and forth. Horse mussels lie half buried on the bottom and filter the water they ingest. Sometimes inedible foreign objects enter the shells and can't be expelled. Grains of sand can become lodged between mantle and shell. These foreign objects become encapsulated in a kind of calcium shell – and that's the seed of a pearl. As time passes, more and more calcium layers are deposited on the pearl. These calcium layers contain substances that make the outer surface shiny, colorful and smooth. This is the "mother" of the pearl. In some kinds of mollusks and snails, the mother of pearl is quite beautiful. In our domestic mussel and horse mussel, unfortunately, it is matte and colorless, and the pearls are rarely beautiful enough to be of any value. But large horse mussel and common mussel pearls can have a sentimental value as a souvenir for the "lucky" finder.

Brushworm tubes, red crustose algae-which produce calcium - and bryozoans cover the shell of the horse mussel. These are all decorative, but scrub and rinse well before preparation. There can be sand and mud in between all the different growth, and this should be removed before preparation.

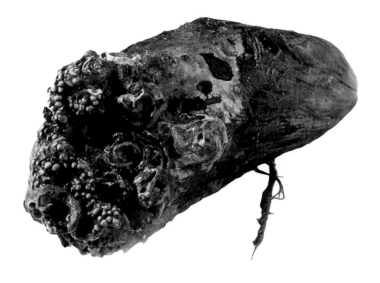

HORSE MUSSELS AU GRATIN

8 horse mussels
1 shallot
1 tablespoon butter
1 teaspoon chopped parsley
1 teaspoon chopped chives

Scrub mussels. Bring 3 dl (1 1/4 cups) water to a boil in a saucepan. Add mussels, cover and cook until all have opened and meat is firm. Remove mussels from cooking liquid and cool a little before removing from shells (see page 66). Chop.

Clean and mince garlic and shallot and sauté in butter. Stir in parsley, chives and mussel pieces.

Vegetables

1/2 carrot
1/2 celery stalk
1 small red onion
1 tablespoon butter
salt and pepper

Clean and shred vegetables. Sauté in butter until soft. Season with salt and pepper. Dry 8 shells and fill with vegetables.

Sauce

1/2 shallot
1 tablespoon butter
1/2 dl (3 1/2 tablespoons) white wine
1 dl (scant 1/2 cup) whipping cream
3 egg yolks
2 teaspoons Dijon mustard
1 teaspoon chopped dill

Clean and chop shallot and sauté in butter. Add white wine and reduce until only a few drops remain. Add cream and bring to a boil. Whisk egg yolks lightly in a bowl which withstands heat. Whisk in boiling cream, then add mustard and dill. Season with salt and pepper.

Preheat oven grill. Place vegetable-filled shells in an ovenproof dish. Top with shellfish. Pour over sauce and grill until golden. Serve with hearty bread.

DEEP-FRIED HORSE MUSSELS WITH LENTIL-SPINACH SALAD

8 steamed and cleaned horse mussels
(see page 66)
8 satay sticks
tempura batter (see page 41)

Lentil-Spinach-salad

100 g (1 1/4 dl) green lentils
2 small garlic cloves
1 tablespoon butter
100 g (4 oz) spinach, rinsed of all
sand
2 tablespoons chopped chives
salt and pepper

Bacon Vinaigrette

100 g (4 oz) slab bacon
1 tablespoon olive oil
1 shallot, minced
1/2 dl (3 1/2 tablespoons) balsamic
vinegar
2 tablespoons chopped chives
4 thin bacon slices
corn oil

Thread mussels chunks onto each satay stick and refrigerate. Prepare tempura batter.

Cook lentils in lightly salted water until tender. Drain. Crush garlic and sauté in butter until golden. Add spinach and steam until all liquid has evaporated. Add lentils and season with chives, salt and pepper.

Dice bacon and sauté in oil. Add shallot with vinegar and chives.

Preheat oven to 160ºC (320ºF). Fry bacon slices until crisp, about 35 minutes. Drain on paper towels.

Heat oil to 170ºC (350ºF). Just before serving, dip mussel sticks in tempura batter. Deep-fry until golden and drain on paper towels.

Toss lentils with bacon vinaigrette. Arrange mounds of salad on four plates. Top with mussel sticks and garnish with bacon.

SPRING ROLLS WITH HORSE MUSSELS AND JUMBO SHRIMP

Filo pastry is very versatile. You can wrap and fry just about anything. But the filling must not be too wet, and all ingredients should have the same cooking time. Here is a recipe for crispy spring rolls with horse mussels and tiger prawns. Serve with Indonesian satay sauce and pickled white daikon radish. You can also use thin slices of turnip or regular radish instead of daikon.

Spring rolls

8 steamed and cleaned horse mussels
(see page 66)
150 g (5 oz) raw tiger prawns
(or shrimp)
without shells
1 large garlic clove
1 teaspoon chopped fresh ginger
2 tablespoons olive oil
3 drops sesame oil
1 teaspoon lime juice
salt
2 teaspoons chopped coriander
4 filo sheets
corn oil

Cut each mussel into 4 pieces. Clean and devein prawns. Cut into chunks the same size as mussels and combine. Sauté garlic and ginger in oil until shiny. Season with sesame oil, lime juice, salt and fresh coriander. Stir into mussels and shrimp. Divide among filo sheets. Fold over sides and roll up. Moisten ends with water to seal. Heat oil to 170ºC (350ºF). Just before serving, deep-fry until golden, about 5 minutes. Drain on paper towels.

Pickled daikon radish

200 g (7 oz) daikon white radish
1/2 dl (3 1/2 tablespoons) rice vinegar
1/2 teaspoon minced fresh ginger
(do not use powdered)
1/2 red chile, in thin rings
4 garlic cloves, thinly sliced
2 tablespoons chopped coriander

Shred radish. Combine remaining ingredients. Marinate radish overnight.

Satay sauce

1 tablespoon peanut butter
1/2 garlic clove
1/2 dl (3 1/2 tablespoons) coconut milk
(do not use coconut cream)
1/2 dl (3 1/2 tablespoons) chicken stock
3 tablespoons soy sauce
2 teaspoons sugar
salt (optional)

Bring all ingredients to a boil, stirring constantly. Simmer until thick.

Serve spring rolls with radish and sauce in a small bowl alongside.

BEVERAGE SUGGESTION

Drink with green tea, preferably in pretty Chinese cups.

COCKLES AND CLAMS
not just playthings for children

Cardium edule is cockle in Latin. *Cardium* means heart, and *edule*, edible. "The edible heart" is tasty, beautiful food. Their Norwegian name is a literal translation from the Latin. We've all seen this round, heart-shaped, white shell on the beach. We collected and played with them as children. As we walk along the coast, we still bend over and pick them up and put them in our pockets – they are good to hold.

We have also learned to dig a little in the sand. Wherever there are empty shells, there are also live ones around. At least nearby. Cockles like soft sand and muddy bottoms. They are robust and tolerate some fresh water well – they survive admirably in places where other bivalves cannot, in places with flat tides, fresh water and exposure to rain and frost. We can find some on the surface of the sand and some half-buried, while most are just under the surface of the sand. They have a strong foot to dig with, and they can move around. Most of the time they lie quietly, with their two siphons stretched up into the water. They draw in water through the one, filter out the edible particles, and then they pump water and waste out through the other. Crouch down on the flat part of the beach where the water is only a few inches deep and watch them.

The common cockle is a common and popular species in most of Europe. Cockles are found along the entire Norwegian coast. The density of cockles in the sand can be impressive, and on large sandy surfaces, there can be tons of them, hidden from sight. In Norway, we have just barely begun to take advantage of this resource, and we have little experience in using cockles. But we can learn from how they are treated in other European countries. As always, it pays to harvest correctly. Before we know how productive the Norwegian cockle populations are, it is a good strategy to take only the largest shells and leave the small ones.

Many species of clams have very decorative shells. Clams can be a pleasure for both eye and palate.

In small quantities, we can dig them up with a small shovel. We usually take a trowel from the garden. It takes up almost no space and does the job really well. Those who harvest for sale use rakes and a grip – and they wonder how to make their harvesting methods more efficient. It is usually acceptable to pick cockles and clams for private use, but it is important to remember that anything found on a dry beach is considered a product of the wilderness, not of the sea, according to Norwegian law. The harvesting is therefore reserved for the owner of the land.

Clams - exciting, hidden treats

While digging, we also find other kinds of bivalves. Those living buried in the sand are referred to by the general term clams.

Soft-shell clams are quite common, and we find them spread out among the cockles on sandy and clay bottoms, at the bottom of the tidal zone. They sit a little deeper in the sand and have to be dug out with a larger shovel or grip. This species has an oblong shell with a matte, dirty white, rather irregular surface. The meat has a little firm texture and is best when chopped up.

In some places, we can find small amounts of other clams – like carpet shells, venus shells and dog cockles. They sit about as far down in the sand as the common cockles, but they do not like fresh water, so they are found away from streams and places where fresh water flows in, usually a little farther out where they can be exposed to waves. They can be recognized by their slightly oval, symmetrical shell halves, which feature beautiful stripe or zig-zag patterns in some species. These clams are delicious. In southern Europe, they are very popular and bring a good price. Some are even farmed.

In Norway, the availability of cockles and clams is quite limited. Packages of live cockles are available in certain places, but often we have to dig for them ourselves. When they are available, those who market cockles deliver them to wholesalers, so it is possible to inquire. Most of the time, they go to hotels and restaurants.

Preparation - first get rid of the sand

Purchased cockles and clams are ready to use. If you dig them yourself, you have to consider the life style of the buried shells. When they filter, they take in water and edible particles, but also a great deal of sand. It is gritty and annoying to eat. The shells expel the sand when placed in clean seawater. Let the shells hang in a net in the sea, or put them in a tub with clean, cool seawater, and change it now and then. When the shells have expelled the sand, they are ready to use. With the exception of soft shell clams, these bivalves can be eaten raw. That is quite common in southern Europe. Most of the time, we steam them before using them in recipes. In soft shell clams, we cut out the siphon. Otherwise, the entire soft parts of both clams and cockles are eaten.

Dishes with cockles and clams

Cockles and clams are very versatile. Many species are decorative and delicious served raw on a platter or combined with other kinds of seafood in stews and soups. These recipes give an idea of the possibilities:

The prickly cockle is easy to recognize by the barbs on its shell. It is found in deeper waters than the common cockle.

Venus shells are both beautiful and delicious. Their shells often feature a zig-zag pattern.

Soft shell clams have a matte, dirty white exterior and long siphons. They are found all along the Norwegian coast.

COCKLES WITH PLUM TOMATOES AND PASTA

Shellfish and pasta are a fine combination with loads of possibilities. Here we have used cockles, any type of bivalves works in this dish.

1 kg (2 1/4 lb) cockles
2 shallots
1 garlic glove
3 tablespoons olive oil

4 plum tomatoes
fresh sage and/or basil

250 g (8-9 oz) fresh pasta
6 tablespoons olive oil
salt and pepper

Place cockles in cold running water for 15-20 minutes. Scrub and rinse well, removing all sand. Clean and chop shallot and garlic. Sauté in olive oil in a saucepan. Add cockles, cover and steam until all have opened.

Scald and peel tomatoes. Halve and remove seeds with a spoon. Cut into wedges. Chop herbes. Add to a saucepan with cockles and heat.

Cook pasta in lightly salted water about 3 minutes. Drain, then stir in oil. Pour over cockles and mix well. Season with salt and pepper.

COCKLES WITH BAKED TOMATOES AND WHITE BEANS

In this dish, we have combined dried ham and white beans – a rather unusual, but exciting combination. A perfect hot dish for a cold winter meal. Not exactly an appetizer, it functions well as a supper dish, when quantities are increased and it is served with a hearty bread.

White beans

3/4 dl (1/3 cup) dried white beans
1 carrot
4 celery stalks
1 onion
1 carlic clove
water or mild chicken stock
salt and pepper
8 thin slices of air-dried ham

Soak beans in a saucepan in water to cover overnight. Drain. Coarsely chop carrot, celery, onion and garlic and add to beans with enough water or stock to cover ingredients by about 4 cm (1 1/2"). Bring to a boil, cover and simmer until all ingredients are tender, about 30 minutes. Season with salt and pepper. Cut ham into thin strips and add during the last minute of cooking time.

Tomatoes

12 small very ripe tomatoes
1 garlic clove
4 tablespoons (1/4 cup) olive oil
thyme leaves
salt and pepper

Preheat oven to 120°C (250°F). Remove stems and halve horizontally. Place in an ovenproof dish, cut side down. Peel and thinly slice garlic. Place on tomatoes. Drizzle oil over and sprinkle with thyme, salt and pepper. Bake 25-30 minutes.

Cockles

3 kg (6 1/2 lb) cockles
1/2 teaspoon chopped fresh thyme
1 dl (1/2 cup) white wine

extra virgin olive oil
chopped fresh parsley

Place cockles in cold running water for 15-20 minutes. Scrub and rinse well. Place in a saucepan with thyme and white wine, cover and steam until all have opened. Mix into beans. Arrange cockles and beans on plates with tomatoes alongside. Drizzle with oil and sprinkle with parsley.

BEVERAGE SUGGESTION

Beer is good with this dish.

WOK VEGETABLES WITH OYSTER SAUCE AND FRIED COCKLES

This fresh, colorful Asian-inspired dish is flavored with oyster sauce. It is a fine flavor enhancer. Try it also in a dip for raw shellfish.

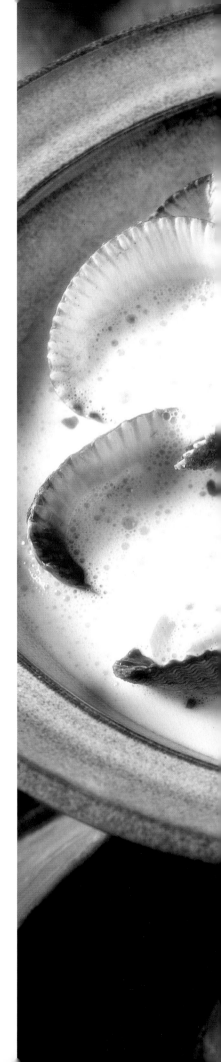

Cockles

2 kg (4 1/2 lb) cockles
12 satay sticks

Place cockles in cold running water for 15-20 minutes. Scrub and rinse well. Place in a hot, dry pan and cover. Steam until all have opened. Remove meat from shells. Thread 4-5 cockles onto each satay stick.

Breadcrumbs

1/4 loaf white bread
1/2 garlic clove
1 tablespoon chopped chives
1 tablespoon chopped parsley
4 tablespoons (1/4 cup)
all-purpose flour
1 egg, lightly beaten
4 tablespoons (1/4 cup) oil

Prepare breadcrumbs (see basic recipes page 109) with garlic and herbs and place on a plate. Dip cockle sticks first in flour (be sure to shake of excess flour), then in egg and last in breadcrumbs. Place on paper towels and refrigerate until just before serving time. Fry in oil until golden.

Vegetables

1 broccoli stalk
1/2 red chile pepper
1 carrot
1 red onion
1 red bell pepper
oil
salt and pepper
2 tablespoons oyster sauce

Cut broccoli into small florets/slices. Cook in lightly salted water for 1 minute. Plunge immediately into cold water. Drain. Mince chile, slice carrot and red onion, and cut pepper into strips. Sauté quickly in oil in a hot wok or frying pan. Stir in oyster sauce.

Arrange vegetables on plates with cockle sticks alongside.

COCKLE RAGOUT WITH NOILLY PRAT

Noilly Prat is a dry French vermouth which adds flavor to the shellfish stock.

40 cockles

2 shallots
2 tablespoons butter
1 dl (1/2 cup) Noilly Prat or
other vermouth
1 dl (1/2 cup) whipping cream
1 dl (1/2 cup) sour cream
3 tablespoons butter, in pats
salt and pepper
4 tablespoons (1/4 cup) finely
chopped chives

Place cockles in cold running water for 15-20 minutes. Scrub and rinse well. Clean and mince shallot. Sauté in oil in a heavy saucepan until shiny. Add vermouth and reduce until only a few drops remain. Add cockles, cover and steam until all have opened. Remove from pan and place in four soup bowls.

Strain stock and return to pot. Add cream, sour cream and butter. Bring to a boil, but remove from heat as soon as it begins to bubble. Beat with an immersion blender or pour into a food processor and puree until frothy. Season with salt and pepper. Pour over cockles and sprinkle with chives.

GAZPACHO WITH COCKLE-FENNEL SALAD

Gazpacho is a cold Spanish tomato soup. It can be served on its own, but it is even better and more filling with this salad, made with cockles, fennel, celery and red lettuce alongside.

Gazpacho

1 cucumber
2 plum tomatoes
2 teaspoons salt
3 red bell peppers
1 medium red chile pepper
2 teaspoons olive oil
2 celery stalks
1 dl (1/2 cup) olive oil
salt and pepper
lime or lemon juice

Peel cucumber, halve lengthwise and remove seeds. Scald and peel tomatoes. Halve lengthwise and remove seeds. Sprinkle salt on cucumber and tomatoes and drain on paper towels for about 2 hours. Rinse off salt and dry on paper towels.

Preheat oven to 220ºC (425ºF). Halve peppers lengthwise, remove ribs and seeds. Place on an oven sheet, drizzle with oil and bake until skin blisters and peppers are soft, about 10 minutes. Place immediately in a plastic bag to cool. Peel off skin. Peel celery and coarsely chop. Place in a food processor with other ingredients, excluding oil, and puree until smooth. Add oil in a thin stream and season with salt, pepper and lime juice. Refrigerate until ready to serve.

Salad

40 cockles
1 fennel bulb
2 celery stalks
1/6 head red lettuce or other rather bitter green, such as chicory
juice of 1/2 lemon
2 tablespoons extra virgin olive oil
fresh herbs

Place cockles in cold running water for 15-20 minutes. Scrub and rinse well. Place in a hot saucepan, cover and steam until all have opened. Remove and cool. Strain stock and freeze for later use.

Clean and thinly slice fennel and celery. Shred lettuce. If very bitter, soak in ice water for about 30 minutes before shredding. Combine vegetables and cockles and drizzle with lemon juice and oil. Place mounds of salad in the center of a deep bowl and ladle soup all around. Garnish with fresh herbs, such as coriander, basil and chervil. Serve with crisp breadsticks or thin slices of country bread fried in olive oil.

BEVERAGE SUGGESTION

A white Rioja or a dry sherry, such as Manzanilla, suits this dish well.

CLAMS WITH VEGETABLE TERRINE AND WATERCRESS PUREE

You can also use cockles in this dish. Make the terrine a day ahead of time, to save time on the day you plan to serve it.

Terrine

- *2 red bell peppers*
- *2 yellow bell peppers*
- *4 plum tomatoes*
- *2 small leeks or 4 spring onions*
- *1 small zucchini*
- *1 small eggplant*
- *olive oil*
- *1 gelatin sheet*
- *salt and pepper*

- *40 clams (or around 60 cockles)*

Preheat oven to 225ºC (450ºF). Halve peppers, remove stem end and seeds. Place on an baking sheet and bake until skin blisters and peppers are soft, 10-15 minutes. Place immediately in a plastic bag to cool. Remove skin and cut into 2 cm (3/4") strips.

Scald and peel tomatoes. Halve and remove seeds. Cut each half into 6 wedges.

Clean leeks, split lengthwise and rinse well. Boil 2 minutes, then plunge immediately into cold water.

Remove stem end of zucchini and eggplant. Cut into 1 cm (1/2") slices lengthwise and sauté in oil until golden.

Soak gelatin in cold water about 5 minutes. Squeeze out most of the water and melt in a water bath.

Line a 1-liter (4 cup) loaf pan with plastic wrap. Sprinkle plastic with salt and pepper. Place a layer of zucchini in the bottom and brush with gelatin. Layer red pepper, leek, eggplant, yellow pepper and tomato. Season each layer with salt and pepper and brush with gelatin, until everything is used up. Pack plastic wrap over top and place a small weight on the vegetables. Refrigerate overnight.

Place shellfish in cold running water for 15-20 minutes. Scrub and rinse well. Place in a hot saucepan, cover and steam until all have opened. Remove and let cool. Remove meat from shells and reserve. Strain cooking liquid.

Watercress puree

- *1 bunch watercress*
- *shellfish stock*

Pluck leaves from cress and save a few for garnish. Blanch remaining leaves in salted boiling water (3 tablespoons salt per liter/quart). Remove and plunge immediately into ice cold water. Press out some of the water and puree in a food processor with a few tablespoons shellfish stock until smooth.

Arrange slices of terrine on individual plates and arrange shellfish around and on top of terrine. Spoon puree all around and garnish with cress.

RISOTTO WITH CLAMS AND CRISPY PARMA HAM

Risotto is a traditional Italian dish which has become very popular. The risotto itself is described in the basic recipe section. There are many ways to make risotto and the variations are many. Shellfish and fish are often used in risotto along the coast. In this recipe, only bivalves are used. To use as a main dish, increase quantities

Risotto garnish

40 clams (or 60 cockles or a mixture of shellfish)
2 tomatoes
2 large sage leaves, finely chopped
4 slices Parma ham or other flavorful dried ham

Place shellfish in cold running water for 15-20 minutes. Scrub and rinse well. Place in a hot saucepan, cover and steam until all have opened. Remove shellfish from pan and let cool, Remove meat from shells and reserve. Strain cooking liquid and reserve.

Scald and peel tomatoes. Quarter and remove seeds. Dice, then stir in sage.

Preheat oven to 120°F (250°F). Bake ham under pressure so it remains flat: Line a baking sheet with baking parchment. Top with ham, another sheet of parchment and another baking sheet. Bake 30-45 minutes. Drain on paper towels.

Risotto

6–7 dl (2 3/4 cups) light stock (use shellfish cooking liquid plus additional chicken, veal or fish stock)
1 shallot
2 tablespoons butter
250 g (1 1/4 cups) round grain rice
salt and pepper

4 tablespoons (1/4 cup) freshly grated Parmesan cheese
1 tablespoon butter

Reheat cooking liquid. Mince shallot and sauté in butter until shiny. Add rice and stir until shiny. Add enough stock to cover rice. Cook carefully, stirring occasionally, adding hot stock so that rice is always covered. This takes about 20-25 minutes, depending upon type of rice. Never cook rice until it falls apart! Stir in Parmesan and butter and season carefully with salt and pepper. The stock, Parmesan and butter are all salty, so it may not need additional salt.

Just before serving, sauté clams lightly in butter and add tomatoes and sage.

Arrange mounds of risotto on four plates, sprinkle with shellfish and top with sage, tomato and ham slices.

OTHER EDIBLE BIVALVES

RAZOR CLAMS

Razor clams are an unusual sight. They look just like long razors. They are found along the coast, as far north as Troms, but stocks in many places are rather scarce, so most of us do not see these shells very often. They are buried in the sand with their siphons up in the water. If a diver comes upon a field of razor clams, a great number of them can be very close together. When they have expelled their sand, razor clams can be quite tasty.

OCEAN QUAHOG

The ocean quahog is found along the entire coast of Norway, from shallow water to a depth of many hundred meters. It sits almost completely buried on the bottom. The quahog grows slowly, and it can live to a ripe old age – some more than two hundred year old specimens have been found. The Ocean quahog has a thick, compact shell with a horny outer layer which changes from brown in a young specimen to black in an old one. In the olden days, these were harvested and used as bait, along with horse mussels. Old large shells have hard, tough meat, and must be ground up to be used. The small ones are better and can be used in recipes calling for clams. Quahogs are used in the US in clam chowder. There will never be a great market for these shells in Norway, but they can be an interesting secondary catch from the harvest of scallops and horse mussels.

FILE SHELL

File shells are found all along the Norwegian coast as far as the Lofoten island. They are unmistakeable, with their long, orange tentacles. They are found in both shallow and deep water. A relative, the great file shell, which can grow to more than 15 cm (7”), is found deep in the ocean. We have not tasted them, but we have heard that they are delicious.

SNAILS

widespread and unappreciated

In Norway, snails as food are hard to classify. We are not used to eating them, and in our focus on bivalves, crustaceans and other seafood, we tend to forget about them. It is completely different in other parts of the world. In the far east, the abalone snail and the conch are among the most expensive delicacies. In this book, it seems only right to expand the topic a little to include our most important edible sea snails. The whelk and the periwinkle are good seafood and almost never used in Norway.

Whelk

The whelk is common in shallow water, along the entire coast and almost everywhere. It also thrives on a soft bottom. It operates as both a predator and as a scavenger. We can often find it in crab traps and fish pots, where it has crept in – attracted by the remains or smell of dead fish. The whelk can grow as large as 11 cm (4 1/2"), and it has a large, powerful, white foot which is edible. It is most common to cook the snails in court bouillon and let them cool. Either they are served whole in their shells or they are cleaned. The snail is pulled out of its shell and the operculum, the "nail" covering the entrance, as well as the brown innermost spiral, the digestive system, are removed. The white muscle which remains is quite hard in texture, but it has a good flavor.

Periwinkle

Along the smooth rocks by the water and in the tidal zone, we are treading in food all the time – small periwinkles. As children we used to use them as bait for small fish and crabs as we hung over the edge of the quay and got sunburned on our backs. Gray and unprepossessing, but numerous. These are tough little critters which live through drought, sun, rain and frost. When the tide covers them, they move around

A whelk on its journey over stones, gravel and sand – over a species-rich ocean floor, among bivalves and snails, sea anemones and starfish. Who will become the whelk's next meal?

and feed. When the tide is out, they attach themselves to the sea floor and enclose themselves with the operculum to keep from drying out.

In central Europe, periwinkles are popular on platters of seafood. In France, consumption of periwinkles is so great that they must be imported to satisfy demand. They are usually cooked in court bouillon and served as a starter or along with other seafood. The snail is pulled out of the shell after

cooking and cooling, and everything is eaten.

Limpets

Limpets are familiar to everyone who travels along the sea line. They are common, and often visible where they sit like tiny volcanoes, suction to the rock. Many ask if they are edible. The answer is a qualified yes, but they are tough as nails. Most of the edible part is a powerful foot which the snail uses as a suction cup against a surface. It is more useful ground up as a flavoring in a soup than on its own.

DEEP-FRIED WHELKS

This method of preparation can be used with all kinds of seafood. By using different dips, you can make an exciting meal with depth and contrast.

1 kg (2 1/4 lb) whelks
court bouillon
(see basic recipes page 106)

Batter
2 dl (3/4 cup) all-purpose flour
2 dl (3/4 dl) beer
salt and pepper
oil

Suggestions for dip
2 tablespoons mayonnaise
(see basic recipes page 106)
5 drops hot pepper sauce
1 teaspoon chopped flat-leaf parsley
2 tablespoons tomato concassé
(see basic recipes page 109)

Scrub and rinse whelks well. Simmer in court bouillon about 30 minutes. Remove hard operculum ("fingernails") covering entrance to shells, then remove meat. Remove the innermost, spiral part which contains digestive system. Return to court bouillon and simmer 30 more minutes.

Combine flour, beer, salt and pepper and let rest up to 10 minutes. Heat oil to 170°C (350°F). Dip whelks in batter and deep-fry until golden. Drain on paper towels. Mix dip and serve alongside.

CREAMED WHELKS WITH GINGER, SPRING ONIONS AND TOMATO CONCASSÉ

1 kg (2 1/4 lb) whelks
1 litre (quart) court bouillon
(see basic recipes page 106)

3 tomatoes
2 1/2 cm (1") cube fresh ginger
1 shallot
1 1/2 dl (2/3 cup) whipping cream
4 spring onions

1 tablespoon chopped flat-leaf parsley
salt and pepper
chopped chives

Cook and clean whelks as described in previous recipe.

Scald and peel tomatoes. Halve and remove seeds. Cut into strips. Chop ginger and shallot and simmer with 4 tablespoons (1/4 cup) cooking liquid and cream until 1/2 of the original amount remains. Mince spring onion and add along with tomato (save a little for garnish) and parsley. Season with salt and pepper. Add whelks and heat carefully. Garnish with chives. Serve immediately.

WHELKS WITH GREEN CURRY MAYONNAISE

20 whelks
1 litre (quart) court bouillon
(see basic recipes page 106)

1 teaspoon green curry paste
2 tablespoons chopped fresh coriander
1 dl (scant 1/2 cup) mayonnaise
(see basic recipes page 106)

1 tablespoon chopped fresh ginger
2 garlic cloves
1 teaspoon chopped green chile
1/2 dl (3 1/2 tablespoons) olive oil
4 satay sticks

Cook and clean whelks as described in first recipe. Stir curry paste and coriander into mayonnaise. Let steep one hour.

Sauté ginger, garlic and chile in oil 20-30 seconds. Add whelks and sauté quickly. Thread onto satay sticks and place over small bowls of mayonnaise.

FRUITS OF THE SEA
– raw and cooked shellfish

On the French Atlantic coast, a typical "plateau de fruits de mer" contains cooked shellfish such as crab, Norway lobster, two varieties of shrimp, raw oysters, mussels, cockles and clams, along with cooked whelks and periwinkles. More exclusive versions also include half a lobster per person. All these ingredients can be obtained fresh in Norway. Harvest and buy whatever you like and invite your best friends for a local seafood platter. Vary the platter according to the season and availability of ingredients. On a fine autumn evening, you might want to give crab pride of place, in winter you will want oysters and perhaps lobster in the spotlight. During the rest of the winter and into spring, different bivalves are at their best. Midsummer is low season for all shellfish, making assembly of a platter more difficult.

Count on the following amounts per person: 1/2 crab or lobster, a couple of Norway lobster if you can find them (make sure they're fresh), a few shrimp, a selection of oysters, mussels, clams, cockles, whelks and a handful of periwinkles. Think about your guests. Add a little more for hearty eaters. Serve crustaceans freshly cooked and cooled. Divide crab and/or lobster into two or four. Serve oysters raw, and you can do that with other bivalves, too. Most Norwegians prefer steamed shellfish, so it's not certain that your guests will appreciate them served raw for the first time. Cook whelks and periwinkles in court bouillon (see basic recipes) and cool before serving. Top it all off with sea urchins, opened to expose the roe, if you can get them.

Serve with fresh bread, light and dark, in thin slices, mayonnaise, a dip or two – check out the recipes for raw oysters – lemon wedges and a pepper mill. Set the table with forks, claw crackers, lobster forks and snail picks. Arrange on plates, preferably at different heights. Serve crustaceans, bivalves and snails on ice and decorate with seaweed.

Place a pitcher of ice cold water with lemon on the table and choose a wine you know your guests will enjoy – preferably a couple of choices. Select wine for oysters, but make sure that the wine will go with the most flavorful, richest and sweetest delicacies on the table – most probably the crab. A good Chablis, Sancerre, white Bordeaux or a Pinot Gris should be fine. Do not use too full-bodied or sweet wines, as these will clash with the snails and raw shellfish. Take your time over the meal and experience that shellfish are "good time food"!

A cool, inviting toast - to the richness of our coast, to steaming, newly cooked lobster, fried scallops, colorful horse mussels, fresh, salty and sweet oysters, sea urchins and snails. The next toast is to teamwork and to the pleasure of working with the best Norwegian nature can offer.

SOUPS
– made of and with shellfish

The broth which forms when we steam shellfish – and the cooking liquid from crustaceans – are wonderful bases for soups and sauces. The basic recipes at the back of the book contain some recipes for stock. If you save the stock from shellfish meals, make small batches of stock from shrimp and lobster shells, and freeze them, you will always have stock available. Shellfish stock can be too salty, so always taste – and dilute, if necessary.

Shellfish are well-suited to soups. Mussels, horse mussels and oysters can be ground in a food processor and used as a thickener as well as a flavoring agent in soups. All kinds of mollusks can be used in soups, on their own or combined with crustaceans and fish. Let your imagination be your guide. Make sure that shellfish which are to be added to soups and stews do not boil along with the broth. They should be added at the end.

We have chosen a couple of "classics" as well as a few new suggestions for exciting shellfish soups.

EASY MUSSEL SOUP

You can use any kind of shellfish in this soup, or even a combination, such as cockles, clams and mussels.

2 kg (2 1/4 lb) fresh mussels

3 garlic cloves
2 tablespoons butter
1 dl (1/2 cup) full-fat milk
1 dl (1/2 cup) whipping cream
3 tablespoons dairy sour cream
3 tablespoons cold unsalted butter
pepper
3 tablespoons chopped chives

Scrub mussels. Clean and mince shallot and garlic. Sauté in butter until soft but not brown. Add mussels, cover and steam until all have opened, 2-3 minutes. Remove mussels and cool slightly. Remove meat from shells and reserve. Strain cooking liquid and bring to a boil with milk and cream. Pour into a blender or food processor and add sour cream and cold butter. Purée until frothy, or use an immersion blender. Heat through, but do not allow to boil (or the sour cream will make the soup curdle). Season with pepper (the mussels add enough salt). Divide mussels among four soup bowls and ladle over soup. Garnish with chives.

OYSTER SOUP WITH WATERCRESS

Oysters are also good in soup. You can make it with shellfish stock enriched with cream and flavored with lime. Add steamed oysters just before serving. Here is another easy recipe for a delicious oyster soup:

20 oysters
2 dl (1 cup) fish stock
1 dl (1/2 cup) whipping cream
1 shallot, minced
1 dl (1/2 cup) crème fraiche or
dairy sour cream
2 tablespoons cold unsalted butter
lemon juice
cayenne pepper
salt and pepper
watercress

freshly ground pepper

Open oysters and remove from shells. Set 8 aside for garnish. Use remaining in soup.

Bring stock, cream, shallot and crème fraiche to a boil (if using dairy sour cream, add with butter). Beat in cold butter, a little at a time. Pour into a food processor. With machine on, add remaining 12 oysters and puree until smooth. Add lemon juice, cayenne, salt and pepper to taste. If soup is too thick, add a little stock or water.

Combine remaining oysters with watercress and pepper. Divide mixture among four soup bowls and ladle over soup.

Serve with home-made bread or toast.

BEVERAGE SUGGESTION

Serve water with lemon/lime, mineral water, light beer or a dry or semi-dry white wine – all according to the occasion.

SPINACH-COCKLE SOUP WITH TOMATO-HERB BREADED COCKLES

2 kg (4 1/2 lb) cockles
1 dl (1/2 cup) white wine

Scrub cockles free from sand. Steam in white wine until they open. Cool, covered, so they don't dry out.

100 g (4 oz) fresh spinach

Clean and rinse spinach well. Blanch in boiling lightly-salted water. After spinach deflates, cook about 30 seconds more. Remove with a slotted spoon and plunge into cold water. When cooled, squeeze out as much water as possible.

Breaded cockles

25 g (3/4 dl, 1/3 cup)
dried tomatoes
2 dl (3/4 cup) warm water
cleaned cockles
100 g (1 1/4 cups) breadcrumbs
1 teaspoon minced basil leaves
1 teaspoon minced
tarragon leaves
all-purpose flour
2 eggs, lightly beaten

Soak tomatoes in warm water about 10 minutes. Squeeze out as much water as possible and mince. Remove cockles from shells and strain cooking liquid. Place breadcrumbs, tomatoes and herbs in a food processor and run until finely ground. Dip cockles first in flour, then in egg, and last in crumbs. Just before serving, fry in oil until golden.

Soup

2 shallots
2 garlic cloves
oil
cooking liquid from cockles
2 dl (1 cup) fish stock
2 dl (1 cup) whipping cream
3 tablespoons unsalted butter
grated nutmeg
salt and pepper

oil

Clean, peel and mince shallot and garlic. Sauté in oil in a large saucepan until shiny. Add strained stock with fish stock and cream. Simmer 5-10 minutes. Stir in butter. Just before serving, bring to a boil and add spinach. Simmer one minute, then pour into a food processor and puree until bright green and frothy, or use an immersion blender. Season with nutmeg, salt and pepper. Serve with breaded cockles and garnish with fresh herbs.

BEVERAGE SUGGESTION

Serve a glass of good white wine from Alsace, dry Tokay or dry sherry – preferably a Manzanilla.

CIOPPINO

Cioppino is a relatively spicy soup from Italy by way of San Francisco, possibly a version of the classic French bouillabaisse. It is good on a cold day.

You can substitute any kind of fish, shellfish and vegetables for those listed.

100 g (4 oz) mussels
100 g (4 oz) cockles
2 1/2 dl (1 cup) white wine
200 g (8 oz) shrimp in their shells
1 large onion, minced
5 garlic cloves, minced
2 dl (1/3 cup) olive oil
2 spring onions, minced
2 green bell peppers, cubed
250 g (9 oz) drained canned tomatoes
4 plum tomatoes, diced
2 bay leaves
1/2 teaspoon oregano
1/2 teaspoon marjoram

100 g (4 oz) white fish fillet, in 3 cm (1 1/4") cubes
2 tablespoon chopped parsley
2 tablespoon chopped fresh basil

Make stock with mussels, cockles and white wine. Clean shrimp and make stock with shells, a little water and shellfish stock. Simmer 10 minutes. Strain. Sauté onion and garlic in oil until soft. Add spring onion, peppers and dried herbs. Sauté 2-3 minutes more. Add canned and fresh tomatoes. Simmer over medium heat about 30 minutes. Season to taste. Recipe can be prepared up to this step in advance.

Just before serving, add fish to soup and bring to a boil. Add shellfish and shrimp and heat through. Sprinkle with parsley and basil right before serving.

BEVERAGE SUGGESTION

Serve with ice water with lime, beer, a cool white wine with a little residual sweetness or a light, young and lightly chilled red wine.

PROVENÇALE SOUP

Saffron and fennel are the most important seasonings in this hearty soup, and they add their own distinctive flavor. This soup is on the menu along the entire Mediterranean coast, but especially in Marseilles. It is practical to make a big batch. This recipe is enough for 6 or 8 servings.

Soup

1 1/2 kg (3 1/2 lb) white fish fillets, several types if desired
750 g (1 3/4 lb) assorted shellfish (mussels, clams, cockles)
1 green bell pepper
1/2 dl (3 1/2 tablespoons) olive oil
1 small onion, minced
4 garlic cloves, chopped
white of 1 leek, chopped
500 g (1 1/4 lb) ripe tomatoes, quartered
2 teaspoons fennel seed
2 teaspoon dried thyme
a few threads saffron
3 parsley sprigs
1 bay leaf
2 litres (8 cups) fish stock
salt and freshly ground pepper

Rouille

3 garlic cloves, coarsely chopped
2–3 red chiles, halved and cleaned
1/2 teaspoon coarse sea salt
3 slices white bread, crusts removed
2 dl (3/4 cup) olive oil

18 baguette slices
grated Jarlsberg or Swiss cheese

Clean, rinse and dry fish fillets. Cut into chunks. Quarter bell pepper, remove seads and cut into strips.

Heat oil in a pot (about 6 liters/1 1/2 gallons). Add onion, garlic, leek and pepper. Stir-fry about 2 minutes. Add tomatoes, fennel, thyme, saffron, parsley, bay leaves and fish. Stir fry one minute. Cover and simmer over low heat for about 10 minutes.

Bring stock to a boil and add. Season with salt and pepper, cover and simmer over low heat for about 20 minutes.

Rouille

Puree garlic, chile and salt in a food processor. Crumble bread and add. With motor running, add oil in a thin stream until mixture is emulsified.

Remove shellfish, puree soup in a blender or food processor. Rinse pot and strain soup back into pot. Toast baguette slices and serve alongside with bowls of grated cheese and rouille. You can also spread baguette slices with rouille and place them in soup bowls before ladling over soup.

BEVERAGE SUGGESTION

Drink anything you like with the soup – a bone-dry white wine in the summer, maybe a light Italian or southern French red wine in the winter – and ice water.

CLAM CHOWDER IN A BREAD BOWL

Clam chowder is a classic shellfish soup from the US made with clams, fish and vegetables. This dish works well with Norwegian ingredients. Try it with other kinds of shellfish. You can also make it with chopped quahogs (see page 85).

40 clams
1 large carrot
3 large potatoes
1 small leek
200 g (8 oz) white fish fillet
(haddock, pollack or cod)
1 liter (4 cups) water

Place clams in running water for 15-20 minutes. Scrub well. Place in a hot saucepan, cover and steam until all clams have opened. Remove clams from stock and let cool slightly. Remove from shells and reserve. Strain stock and reserve.

Peel carrot and potatoes and cut into 1 cm (1/2") cubes. Cook in water until tender, about 15 minutes. Split leek lengthwise and rinse well. Cut into 1 cm (1/2") slices. Cube fish. Just before potatoes and carrots are ready, add leek and fish. Strain cooking water into a bowl and reserve.

Stock

2 tablespoons butter
3 tablespoons all-purpose flour
1 dl (1/2 cup) whipping cream
cooking liquid from clams and
vegetables
salt and pepper
2 tablespoons chopped parsley

4 large hard rolls, tops cut off and
crumbs hollowed out, so only hard
shell remains

Melt flour in a saucepan and stir in flour. Let sizzle 3-4 minutes without coloring to remove floury flavor. Gradually whisk in cooking liquid. Season with shellfish stock, salt and pepper. Recipe can be prepared up to this step in advance.

Just before serving, bring stock to a boil. Add cream, vegetables, fish, clams, and parsley. Serve in large hollowed-out rolls or with baguette.

BEVERAGE SUGGESTION

Light beer is good with clam chowder.

COMBINATIONS
of fish and shellfish

There are endless possibilities when combining fish and shellfish. It is difficult to select only a few recipes to represent these dishes, but perhaps one of these might inspire you to try your hand.

RAW MARINATED TROUT WITH OYSTER CREAM

Select the reddest fish, if you are planning to serve it raw. Rainbow trout or char are both good, since the color is often even more intense than with salmon.

300 g (10 oz) boneless trout fillet

Marinade

1/2 teaspoon lemon juice
2 tablespoons olive oil
salt and pepper
a little water (if necessary)

Oyster Cream

3 oysters
1 tablespoon lemon juice
salt and freshly ground pepper
2 tablespoons extra virgin olive oil

Garnish

1 bunch arugula, curly endive or other lettuce
1 tablespoon olive oil
salt and freshly ground pepper
1 tablespoon chopped chives

Cut trout into thin slices lengthwise and place in one layer on a plate. Combine marinade and brush on trout 30-60 minutes before serving. It will turn a lighter color from the acid in the lemon.

Open oysters and loosen from shell. Puree in a food processor with lemon juice, a little water, salt and pepper. With motor running, add oil in a thin stream until emulsified. Adjust seasoning, if necessary.

Wash arugula, dry with paper towels and toss with oil, salt and pepper. Serve trout with a spoonful of oyster cream alongside. Garnish with arugula salad and sprinkle with chives.

PIZZA WITH SCALLOPS AND HALIBUT, BAKED TOMATOES, PARMESAN AND MOZZARELLA

Pizza crust

- *900 g (2 lb) bread flour*
- *5 dl (2 cups) lukewarm water*
- *20 g (3/4 oz) dry yeast*
- *1 tablespoon salt*
- *1 dl (scant 1/2 cup) olive oil*

Scallops

- *6 large scallops*
- *100 g (4 oz) halibut fillet*
- *2 tablespoons olive oil*
- *salt and pepper*

Baked tomatoes

- *30 small tomatoes*
- *1 dl (scant 1/2 cup) olive oil*
- *salt and pepper*
- *5 garlic cloves*
- *4 shallots*
- *small bunch thyme*

Tomato sauce

- *2 garlic cloves*
- *1 shallot*
- *4 tablespoons (1/4 cup) olive oil*
- *1 can (400g, 14 oz) tomatoes*

Garnish

- *2 fresh mozzarella cheeses, sliced*
- *4 tablespoons (1/4 cup) grated fresh Parmesan cheese*
- *extra virgin olive oil*
- *4 tarragon stalks*

Pizza Crust

Combine half the flour, water, yeast and salt until smooth. Stir in oil and remaining flour. Knead well. Cover with plastic wrap and let rise about one hour. Preheat oven to 180°C (350°F). Punch down dough and knead again. Divide into 10 pieces of equal size. Roll out to a thin crust. Bake about 2 1/2 minutes. Cool. Freeze any extra crusts.

Filling

Clean scallops and fish. Cut into thin slices and sauté in oil until almost done. Season with salt and pepper. Preheat oven to 150°C (300°F). Clean garlic, cutting each clove in two. Clean shallots and slice. Place in an ovenproof dish with tomatoes and drizzle oil over. Sprinkle with salt and pepper. Bake about 30 minutes.

Tomato Sauce

Clean and mince garlic and shallots. Sauté in oil until shiny. Add tomatoes and reduce over low heat, stirring often, until thickened.

Preheat oven to 200°C (400°F). Spread tomato sauce on pizza crusts. Top with scallops, fish, baked tomatoes, mozzarella and Parmesan cheese. Bake until filling is hot and crust crisp, about 4 minutes. Drizzle with a little olive oil and garnish with tarragon just before serving.

THYME-SAUTÉED MONKFISH WITH MUSSELS AND COCKLES SERVED WITH NEW CABBAGE AND SAFFRON-PEPPER SAUCE

Shellfish

500 g (1 1/4 lb) cockles
500 g (1 1/4 lb) mussels

Sauce

2 red or yellow bell peppers
1 tablespoon oil
2 shallots
1 dl (1/2 cup) white wine or
dry vermouth
pinch saffron
2 dl (3/4 cup) olive oil
salt and pepper

Cabbage

600 g (1 1/4 lb) early cabbage
water
butter
salt

Baked Potato Wedges

8 almond or other flavorful potatoes
5 garlic cloves
2 shallots
2 fresh thyme branches
(or rosemary, sage or tarragon)
olive oil

Monkfish

800 g (1 3/4 lb) monkfish
4 teaspoons fresh thyme leaves
salt and pepper
2–3 tablespoons olive oil
fresh herbs

Place shellfish in cold running water for 15-20 minutes. Scrub and rinse well. Steam, covered until shells open. Strain cooking liquid and reserve for sauce. Remove meat from shells and reserve.

Sauce

Preheat oven to 240°C (450°F). Quarter peppers, removing stem end and seeds. Brush with oil and bake until skin blisters and pepper is soft, around 10-15 minutes. Immediately place in a plastic bag to cool. Remove skin. Clean and mince shallot and place in a saucepan with wine and saffron. Reduce until half of original amount remains. Pour into a food processor with 2/3 of the baked peppers and puree until smooth. With engine running at lowest speed, add shellfish stock and oil in a thin stream. Reheat carefully just before serving.

Cabbage

Clean cabbage and cut into wedges almost all through to the core. The wedges should still be joined at core. Simmer in water with salt and butter until tender. New cabbage takes less than 10 minutes, ordinary cabbage takes longer.

Potatoes

Preheat oven to 160°C (320°F). Cut potatoes into wedges. Peel and chop garlic and shallot. Toss on an oven tray with potatoes, garlic, shallot and herbs. Bake 25-30 minutes.

Fish

Cut monkfish into four pieces of equal size. Sprinkle with fresh thyme, salt and pepper. Sauté in oil in a very hot frying pan or grill pan until golden and crispy on both sides. Serve with cabbage, baked potato wedges, sauce and shellfish all around. Garnish with fresh herbs such as thyme or flat-leaf parsley.

Most of these basic recipes are elements in the other recipes in this book. In addition to many classics, we have included recipes for sidce dishes which are very useful in many respects – not just when you are preparing dishes with shellfish.

Baked garlic

garlic
coarse sea salt

Preheat oven to 150ºC (300ºF). Cut off the lowest part of the whole garlic. Cover bottom of an ovenproof dish with salt. Place garlic on salt and bake one hour, until cloves are soft. Baked garlic cloves are very useful in all kinds of sauces, dressings and with sautéed vegetables. Store in oil in the refrigerator.

Court bouillon

Court bouillon is an aromatic blend of wine and water to use for cooking fish and shellfish, instead of just lightly salted water. While salt water is neutral, court bouillon adds flavor to the ingredients. Here is one version, but additional flavors, such as lemongrass, fresh ginger, chile or cloves, can be added.

2 dl (scant 1 cup) white wine
1 liter (4 cups) water
4 tablespoons (1/4 cup) salt
1 tablespoon black peppercorns
1/2 onion, sliced
1 bay leaf

Bring all ingredients to a boil and let simmer up to 20 minutes before adding fish or shellfish.

DRESSINGS AND MARINADES

Mayonnaise

Homemade mayonnaise is heavenly. Ready-made is for picnic or panic use. Here are two simple recipes for mayonnaise:

Alternative 1
1 garlic clove
2 egg yolks
1 teaspoon Dijon mustard
1/4 teaspoon salt
1 teaspoon lemon juice or vinegar
1 1/2–2 dl (2/3–3/4 cup) olive oil

Clean and crush garlic and place in a bowl. Whisk in egg yolks, mustard, salt and lemon/vinegar. Whisk in oil, first in drops, then in a thin stream, until emulsified. The mayonnaise should be thick, shiny and smooth. For extra flavor, add saffron or herbs.

Alternative 2
This simple mayonnaise can be made in a food processor. It does not separate and is a good basic recipe which can be flavored with tomato paste, herbs or spice blends.

4 egg yolks
4 teaspoons Dijon mustard
2 tablespoons white wine vinegar
(or lemon juice)
1 dl (scant 1/2 cup) water
2 teaspoons salt
5 dl (2 cups) mild oil (or olive oil)
2 tablespoons chopped fresh
coriander or other fresh herbs

Place all ingredients, excluding oil and herbs, in a food processor and puree for one minute. With motor running, add oil in a thin stream until emulsified. Add coriander and/or other flavorings.

Slightly acidic spicy dressing

Try this as an alternative to purchased cream based dressings. You will discover that even the simplest salad is exciting with it. Homemade dressings and mayonnaise with egg yolks keep only for a short time and have to be stored in the refrigerator.

1 small shallot
2 teaspoons minced red chile pepper
1/2 dl (3 1/2 tablespoons) red wine
vinegar
2 teaspoons Dijon mustard
2 egg yolks
2 teaspoons capers
1 tablespoon chopped sour pickle
1 dl (scant 1/2 cup) sour pickle brine
3–4 dl (1 1/4–1 2/3 cups) corn oil
2 tablespoons chopped chives
2 tablespoons chopped parsley
salt and pepper

Clean and chop shallot. Place in a food processor with chile, vinegar, mustard, egg yolks, capers, pickle and brine and purée until smooth. With motor running, add oil in a thin stream until emulsified. Add herbs and salt and pepper to taste.

Tomato vinaigrette

Use tomato vinaigrette with seafood dishes – both as a marinade for fish and shellfish, as a salad dressing or as a dip.

2 sun-dried tomatoes
2 dl (3/4 cup) water
1 garlic clove
1 shallot
2 tomatoes
1 tablespoon tomato paste
1 dl (scant 1/2 cup) olive oil
2 tablespoons balsamic vinegar
salt and pepper

1 teaspoon shredded fresh basil
1 teaspoon shredded fresh
flat-leaf parsley

Shred dried tomatoes and place in a bowl. Bring water to a boil, pour over tomatoes and let soak 15 minutes. Drain, pressing liquid out of tomatoes. Clean and mince garlic and shallot. Scald, peel and chop tomatoes. Cook sun-dried tomatoes, fresh tomatoes, garlic and shallot together with tomato paste in oil until soft. Transfer to a bowl to cool, then stir in remaining ingredients.

Shellfish marinade

There are many possibilities when making marinades or dips for shellfish. In the chapter on oysters, page 43, there are many recipes for dips/marinades. Use this simple marinade with raw scallops, and other bivalves.

1 shallot
1/2 garlic clove
2 teaspoons chopped red chile pepper
grated zest and juice of 1 lime
1/2 dl (3 1/2 tablespoons) extra
virgin olive oil
1 tablespoon walnut oil
salt and pepper
chopped fresh coriander

Clean and mince shallot and garlic and place in a bowl with chile and lime zest. Whisk in lime juice and both oils. Season with salt, pepper and if necessary, more lime juice. Stir in coriander.

Horseradish cream

Use horseradish cream as a dip or as an accompaniment to fish and shellfish dishes, but remember that it has quite a pronounced flavor.

1/2 dl (3 1/2 tablespoons)
crème fraiche
or dairy sour cream
2 tablespoons milk
1 teaspoon sugar
2 tablespoons grated horseradish
1 teaspoon fresh lime juice
1 tablespoon chopped chives
salt and pepper

Whisk together crème fraiche, milk and sugar. Stir in horseradish, lime juice and chives. Season with salt and pepper.

SAUCES

Beurre blanc

Beurre blanc is a classic French sauce, which is very good with fish and shellfish dishes. True beurre blanc does not contain cream, but a small amount makes the sauce more stable, so it doesn't separate so easily. In addition, it keeps longer.

2 tablespoons minced shallot
2 tablespoons butter
1 dl (scant 1/2 cup) white wine
3 tablespoons whipping cream
125 g (4 1/2 oz) cold unsalted butter,
cubed
salt and pepper

Sauté shallot in butter until soft. Add wine and reduce until 1/3 of the original amount remains. Add cream, bring to a boil and whisk in cubes of butter. Season with salt and pepper.

Clarified butter

Melt butter in a saucepan until it almost reaches the boiling point. Remove scum. Pour off clear liquid, leaving salt and milk residue in pan. The clear liquid is clarified butter. Without milk residue, etc., clarified butter tolerates much higher cooking temperatures than regular butter, making it better for frying and for sauces.

Hollandaise sauce

Hollandaise is another classic sauce which is good with shellfish, fish and light meats. It is a good basic sauce, to which you can add many different flavors.

1 dl (scant 1/2 cup) apple cider
vinegar
pinch pepper
2 tablespoons water
4 egg yolks
400 g (14 oz) clarified butter
(see previous recipe)
fresh lemon juice
salt and pepper

Reduce vinegar and pepper until almost all liquid has evaporated. Add water. Whisk in egg yolks and whisk over a water bath for 4-8 minutes, until yolks are thick and volume has increased 3-6 times original amount. Whisk in clarified butter, little by little. Season with lemon juice, salt and pepper. Add a few drops of water, if sauce is too thick.

PASTA

500 g (3 1/2 – 4 cups) all-purpose flour
10 egg yolks
1 egg
pinch salt
3 drops oil

or

500 g (3 1/2–4 cups) all-purpose flour
11 egg yolks
1 egg

Place all ingredients in a food processor and puree 20 seconds. Knead dough together, pack in plastic wrap and refrigerate at least 2 hours. Remove dough from refrigerator, then roll out to desired thickness. Cut by hand or in a pasta machine. Cook 1-2 minutes.

If you plan to store the pasta, dry it a little, then pack it in plastic wrap. Refrigerate, but if planning to store longer than 24 hours, freeze.

BREAD

The reason many have problems baking bread is that they knead the dough too little, don't let it rise long enough and they bake it at too low a temperature for too little time. Make it a habit to let all doughs rise three times before baking. Sprinkle dough with flour, cover with plastic and let it rise at least one hour each time. Then you will have a bread with more flavor, one which keeps its flavor better, and which lasts longer.

Country bread

1 1/2 liters (6 cups) water
1 1/2 dl (2/3 cup) olive oil
1/2 teaspoon sugar
1 tablespoon salt
2 packets (about 1/2 oz) active dry yeast
2300 g (about 5 lb) all-purpose flour flour for kneading

Combine all ingredients and knead at least 10 minutes. Cover with plastic and let rise until doubled, about 1 hour. Punch down dough, cover with plastic and let rise until doubled, about 45 minutes. Divide dough into four equal pieces and knead lightly. Form each into a bread and place in an oven pan. Sprinkle with flour, cover with plastic and let rise about one hour. Preheat oven to 250°C (450°F). Bake 10 minutes. Reduce oven temperature to 180°C (350°F). Bake large breads one hour more, small ones less. The crust should be crisp.

Bread with sun-dried tomatoes

1 1/4 dl (1/2 cup) milk
2 1/2 dl (1 cup) water
1 package (about 1/2 oz) dry yeast
5 dl (2 cups) all-purpose flour
25 sun-dried tomatoes (shredded and soaked in water)
1/2 dl (3 1/2 tablespoons) olive oil
1 1/4 dl (1/2 cup) semolina (farina)
2 teaspoons salt
4 teaspoons minced fresh oregano
2 tablespoons minced fresh parsley

Prepare as for previous recipe.

Brioche

Brioche is a flavorful French bread made with a lot of butter. It is popular spread with preserves with coffee at breakfast and it's the classic accompaniment to foie gras.

1 tablespoon fresh yeast
2 dl (3/4 cup) warm water
1 1/2 dl (2/3 cup) milk
2 teaspoons salt
2 tablespoons sugar
470 g (2 1/2– 3 cups) all-purpose flour
6 eggs
450 g (1 lb) soft unsalted butter

Dissolve yeast in water. Combine milk, salt and sugar in a bowl. Mix slowly with a dough hook. With motor running, add flour, then yeast mixture. Knead 5 minutes. Add eggs, one at a time. Knead at low spead about 10 minutes more. Add butter in pats, a little at a time. Knead until smooth and elastic. Cover with plastic wrap and let dough rise about 2 hours. Punch down dough, cover with plastic and let rise in refrigerator at least 2 hours, preferably overnight. It's best to let dough rise in refrigerator because the butter has to be cold in order to shape the dough. Wrap dough well if it is stored more than one day. Form into 2 breads and place in greased pans. Cover with plastic and let rise until doubled, about 1 hour. Preheat oven to 200°C (400°F). Bake 30-35 minutes.

BREADCRUMBS

Prepare breadcrumbs as needed. Use white or light bread. Slice bread and remove crusts. It is possible to use 2-3 day old bread or let it sit on the countertop several hours (preferably overnight) before using. Tear into coarse chunks and place in a food processor and run until fine. For extra flavor, process fresh herbs, garlic, fresh Parmesan cheese and other flavor elements with bread.

ACCOMPANIMENTS

Pesto

Pesto is a classic Italian accompaniment with many different uses. Use blanched almonds if you can't get pine nuts. But do grate the Parmesan cheese yourself.

5 dl (2 cups) basil leaves
1 1/4 dl (1/2 cup) olive oil
2 tablespoons pine nuts
2 garlic cloves, crushed
1 1/4 dl (1/2 cup) grated
fresh Parmesan

Purée all ingredients, excluding cheese, in a food processor until almost smooth. It is possible to add cheese at beginning, but then consistency is not as interesting. Pesto was originally made in a morter, and the old method really does yield the best result. Store in the refrigerator.

Anchoiade

This is a kind of anchovy butter. Spread it on toast as a little tidbit before the guests go to the table. This is also good as a topping for baked fish.

50–60 g (2 oz) salted anchovies
2 garlic cloves
1 tablespoon olive oil
2 tablespoons soft butter
1/2 teaspoon lemon juice
4 teaspoons cognac
2 tablespoons crème fraiche
black pepper

Purée anchovies, garlic, olive oil and butter in a food processor until smooth. Stir in remaining ingredients.

Tomato concassé

Tomato concassé is tomato cubes without skin and seeds. Remove stem and cut an "x" in the stem end with a sharp knife. Plunge tomatoes into boiling water for 10-15 seconds and cool quickly. Remove skin and halve or quarter each tomato. Remove seeds with a spoon and dice tomato flesh.

Bruschetta with marinaded tomatoes

Bruschetta is really just a slice of country bread spread with olive oil and garlic and grilled, often under high heat, but as a rule, it is served with a layer of marinated tomatoes.

4 ripe tomatoes
1 garlic clove
1 shallot
2 tablespoons wine vinegar
1 teaspoon tomato paste
salt and pepper
1 dl (1/2 cup) olive oil
good country bread
garlic
extra virgin olive oil
fresh basil

Scald and peel tomatoes as stated in previous recipe, but cut tomatoes into wedges. Clean and mince garlic and shallot and place in a small bowl. Add vinegar, tomato paste, salt and pepper. Whisk in oil in a thin stream until emulsified. Stir in tomato. Let mixture steep at least one hour before serving.

Cut bread into thin slices and fry until crisp in a frying pan or in the oven. Clean garlic and halve. Rub bread with garlic and drizzle with olive oil. Top with marinated tomatoes and garnish with fresh basil. This makes enough for 4-8 slices.

Ratatouille

Ratatouille is a vegetable dish from Provence. Serve it on its own with good bread and olive oil or use as a side dish with meat, fish or shellfish. Sometimes all ingredients are cut into fine cubes, while other times, it is just coarsely chopped. Do it as you like.

1 zucchini
1 eggplant
4 tomatoes
2 bell peppers
2 onions
4 garlic cloves
4 tablespoons (1/4 cup) tomato purée
olive oil
1 dl (scant 1/2 cup) water
salt and pepper
1 teaspoon ground cumin
sugar (optional, if tomatoes are not ripe enough)

Chop vegetables into chunks of equal size (about 1/2 cm (1/4")). Heat olive oil in a frying pan and fry vegetables which take the most time first – onion, garlic, peppers, etc. Add water and simmer slowly until vegetables are soft and all liquid has evaporated. Season with salt, pepper and cumin. If tomatoes are not quite ripe, add 1-2 teaspoons sugar.

Mushroom risotto

Per person
50–60 g (3/4 dl, 1/3 cup) round grain rice
1/2 shallot, minced
butter
2 dl tablespoons white wine
1 1/2 dl (2/3 cup) stock
pepper
1 tablespoon butter
1 tablespoon fresh grated Parmesan or Pecorino cheese
(recipe from Stig Juelsen at NBSD in Stavanger)

mushrooms
butter
salt and pepper
fresh chervil

You need a wide saucepan with an even curve in the corners to reach down to stir the risotto. The stock has to be warm.

Give the guests an extra glass of wine. The guests are supposed to wait for the risotto, not the reverse.

Sauté rice and shallot in butter until soft. Add white wine and reduce until almost evaporated. Add stock a little at a time, stirring constantly. Simmer about 17-20 minutes. Use water if you run out of stock. Scrape the bottom of the saucepan to bring up any starch which has sunk to the bottom and stir into the rice. Add a little more stock right at the end. Season with pepper. Add butter and cheese and stir over low heat about 2 minutes.

Clean and coarsely chop mushrooms. Sauté in butter until golden. Season with salt and pepper. Fold into risotto. Just before serving, garnish with chervil.

Pappa al pomodoro

This tomato-bread soup is from Tuscany, in northern Italy. We can safely say that it tastes better than it looks. This recipe is completely vegetarian, but it tastes fantastic with sautéed scallops or steamed mussels. It is important to use good quality olive oil.

2 kg (4 1/2 lb) ripe tomatoes
1 red onion
1 celery stalk
1 carrot
2 dl (3/4 cup) extra virgin olive oil
1 1/2 kg (3 lb) country bread
3 garlic cloves
chopped fresh basil
salt and pepper

Scald and peel tomatoes as in recipe for tomato concassé on previous page. Cook tomatoes slowly over low heat for about 30 minutes. Crush and strain. Clean and mince onion, celery and carrot. Sauté in half the olive oil. Add tomatoes and bring to a boil.

Slice bread and soak in water a few minutes. Squeeze out water and tear bread into small chunks. Add to tomatoes and simmer about 10 minutes.

Clean and slice garlic and add. Turn off heat and add remaining oil and basil. Season with salt and pepper. Drizzle a little olive oil on top just before serving.

STOCK

Chicken stock

2 kg (4 1/2 lb) chicken bones
4 dl (1 2/3 cups) coarsely chopped
celeriac
2 carrots
1 onion
2 tomatoes
1 garlic clove
1 bay leaf
3 small thyme branches
1 teaspoon black peppercorns
3 liters (12 cups) cold water
salt

Place everything, excluding salt, in a large pot and bring to a boil. Reduce heat and skim well. Simmer about 1 hour. Strain and cool. Season with salt.

Vegetable stock

2 small red onions
4 carrots
1 medium celeriac
4 leeks
2 fennel bulbs
2 red chile peppers
2 garlic cloves
2 tablespoons olive oil
1 bunch thyme
4 small bunches flat-leaf parsley
2 liters (8 cups) water
1 bay leaf
2 tablespoons black peppercorns
lemon juice salt

Coarsely chop vegetables. Sauté onion in oil until soft. Add remaining vegetables and sauté lightly. Add water, bay leaf and pepper and bring to a boil. Reduce heat and skim well. Simmer about 1 hour. Strain and cool. Season with lemon jujice and salt. Let cool.

Shellfish stock

Shells from shrimp, lobster and Norway lobster are too valuable to throw away. If you do not need the stock right away, you should always take the time to make it and then freeze it for later use. If you do not have time on the day you have the shells, just freeze them and make stock, soup or sauce later. If you have some cognac, you can flambé the shells right after browning. That makes the stock taste better, and it loosens all the sweet flavors in the bottom of the pan.

4 1/2 kg (10 lb) shrimp, lobster
and/or Norway lobster shells
oil
1/2 dl (1/4 cup) coarsely chopped
carrot
1 dl (1/2 cup) coarsely chopped
celeriac
1 1/2 dl (2/3 cup) coarsely chopped
onion
2 dl (1 cup) coarsely chopped leek
3 tablespoons tomato paste
2 dl (3/4 cup) white wine
water, chicken stock or fish stock

Crush shells and sauté in oil. Add vegetables and sauté a little more. Stir in tomato paste. Add wine and water/stock to cover and simmer for about 20 minutes. Lowe heat and simmer very slowly for about 30 more minutes. Strain. Use stock as it is or reduce to desired strength.

Mussel stock

1 kg (2 1/4 lb) mussels
4 shallots
oil
3 (1 1/4 cups) white wine

Scrub and rinse mussels well. Shred shallots and sauté in oil until soft. Add mussels and white wine, cover and bring to a boil. Simmer 1-2 minutes, then remove from heat. Strain off stock and use mussels in another dish.

Fish stock

1 kg (2 1/4 lb) white fish with bones
(such as haddock, ling, whiting or
pollack)
1 dl (1/2 cup) coarsely chopped fennel
parsley stalks
4 dl (1 2/3 cup) coarsely chopped
celeriac
1 large tomatoes, quartered
1/2 tablespoon fennel seed
1/2 tablespoon coriander seed
1/2 tablespoon white peppercorns
1 1/2 dl (2/3 cup) white wine
2 1/2 liters (10 cups) cold water
salt

Place all ingredients, excluding salt, in a large pot and bring to a boil. Skim well. Reduce heat and simmer slowly for about 30 minutes. Strain and cool. Season with salt.

SOURCES:

Gaarder, T. and Bjerkan, P. (1934). *Østers and østerskultur i Norge*. a.s. John Grieg Boktrykkeri, Bergen, 96 pages.

Juelsen, S. (1998). *NB Sørensens Dampskibs-expedition*, 140 pages.

Moen, F.E. and Svensen, E. (1999). *Dyreliv i havet. Håndbok i norsk marin fauna*. KOM forlag, 544 pages.

Strand, Ø. and Vølstad, J. H. (1997). *The Molluscan Fisheries and Culture of Norway*. pages 7-24. I: MacKenzie Jr., C.L., Burrell, Jr., V.G., Rosenfield, A. and Hobart, W.L. (red.). The history, present condition, and future of the molluskan fisheries of North and Central America and Europe, Volume 3, Europe. U.S. Dep. Commer., NOAA Tech. Rep. 129. 240 pages. Wiborg, K. F. (1980). *Mat fra sjøen*. J.W. Cappelens Forlag A/S, 144 pages. Wiborg, *K.F. (1946)*. Undersøkelser over oskjellet (Modiola modiolus (L)). I. Alminnelig biologi, vekst og økonomisk betydning. Fiskeridirektoratets skrifter, Serie Havundersøkelser, volum VIII, No.5. a.s John Griegs Boktrykkeri, Bergen, 85 pages.

OUR THANKS TO:

We would like to thank the following for lending us ceramic platters and dishes:
FORMAT applied arts: Gunnar Thorsen pages 20, 31 and 52; Elin Solstad pages 59 and 81; Karin Aasen page 91 and 97; and Erik Lytskjold page 23.
KONTUR applied arts: Anne Bente Totland page 69.
HJERTHOLM applied and decorative arts: Pages 25, 33, 35, 37, 61, 63, 73, 77, 81, 88, 98.
We would also like to thank the Norwegian Department of Fisheries for their support and the Norwegian Seafood Export Council, Inc. and Norshell for their cooperation.

Useful addresses:

Norwegian Seafood Export Council, Inc.	Norshell
9291 Tromsø	St. Olavs Pir 2
www.seafood.no	7010 Trondheim
Tlf. 77 60 33 33	www.norshell.com
	Tlf. 73 87 42 80

Stein Mortensen was born in Bergen in 1961 and earned his PhD in microbiology from the University of Bergen in 1993. He works as a scientist at the Institute of Marine Research in Bergen, primarily researching diseases of shellfish and problems regarding the spread of diseases in the fish and shellfish farming industries. He is project leader of the Marine Research Institute's bivalve research project, and from 1995 through 1998, he was a research coordinator in the "Norwegian Scallop Program". Stein Mortensen is also an author, writer and editor, with many years of experience from both trade publications and the popular press, and he is also an artist and illustrator. He works chiefly in watercolor and pen and ink, both for his own exhibitions as well as freelance, and he illustrates articles and textbooks. He is an enthusiastic forager, and his freezers and refrigerator are always packed with his finds. Active use of fishing pole, net, fish traps and lobster pots, wet suit, shotgun, mushroom basket, berry picker and his own vegetable garden has helped to make it possible for him to be a passionate hobby chef. His special passion for seafood and wine have been the inspiration for this book.

Per Eide was born in 1954, grew up in Sunnmøre on Norway's west coast and studied to be a photographer at West Surrey College of Art and Design in England. He has participated in the spring exhibition of photography, the Vestland exhibition, many group exhibitions, has had six one-man shows, received two stipends and has sold his work both in Norway and abroad. Previously, he worked 12 years as a portrait photographer, but now he works only on location. He started working with underwater photography in 1992 and has been Norwegian and Nordic master in underwater photography three years in a row, in addition to many top placements in the last three world championships in underwater photography. He has illustrated more than 20 books covering a broad range of topics from food and interiors to landscape and town portraits, and right now he is working with several new titles. He also arranges diving expeditions and workshops in underwater photography all around the world, writes articles and works freelance for diving magazines.

Morten Schakenda was born in Gjerdsvika in southern Sunnmøre, on Norway's west coast, and received his education on the school ship "Gann" in Stavanger. He apprenticed at Ulstein Hotel and attended chefs' school in Åndalsnes. After that, he worked at De Fem Stuer at Holmenkollen Park Hotel in Oslo. During the past years, he has worked at a number of restaurants both in Norway and abroad, including Jans Mat og Vinhus (Jan's House of Food and Wine) in Stavanger, and Restaurants D'Artagnan and Bagatelle in Oslo. He took a year off to trawl shrimp in the northern seas, and he has made study tours to France, the United States, Singapore and Hong Kong. From 1992 to 1999, he worked at the Culinary Institute of Norway in Stavanger, the last year as manager. During that time, he was privileged to be able to have about 200 days traveling, about half of that time abroad. Most of these trips were to promote Norwegian fish. He has been a member of the Norwegian national culinary team since 1997 and has participated in both national and international competitions.

He is chef at Terra Bar & Restaurant in Oslo, which opened in the fall of 1999. He is a proud member of the "Breakfast Club" for chefs all over Norway, with sole exclusive right to admit new members.

He loves nature – both sea and mountain, and he paddles a kayak as often as he can – but Morten works hard, as most chefs do – to get enough time for walks in the mountains after a day at sea.

Charles Tjessem was born in 1971. His roots are in Sandnes, near Stavanger, and in spite of his relatively young age, he has a great deal of experience. He began his career washing dishes at Hotel Sverre in Sandnes when he was only 14. He was also allowed to try his hand in the kitchen, and he liked it so much that he decided to become a chef. After he earned his journeyman's papers, he worked in kitchens in Sweden, Denmark and the United States. After that, he worked at De Fem Stuer at Holmenkollen Park Hotel and was souschef at Bagatelle, both in Oslo. After that, he worked at six of Denmark's best restaurants in six months, for experience plus room and board, and with his suitcase always packed. After that, he went back to his home county and was chef at Mortepumpen and co-owner and chef at Restaurant Cartellet. Today, he is a member of the Norwegian national culinary team and manager of the Culinary Institute in Stavanger. This has given him the possibility of working with in the field in a completely different way. The scope, the challenges, the travels and the possibility of learning something new all the time suits him well. He is concerned with quality of ingredients – availability and seasonal variations, and focuses on these conditions at the Culinary Institute. In addition, contests have always been his passion, and he has received many prizes and honors, both as part of the culinary team and on his own. He is also a judge at cooking competitions.